Chandi

Chandi

TINA HUMPHREY

PAN BOOKS

First published in 2012 by Pan Books
an imprint of Pan Macmillan, a division of Macmillan Publishers Limited
Pan Macmillan, 20 New Wharf Road, London N1 9RR
Basingstoke and Oxford
Associated companies throughout the world
www.panmacmillan.com

ISBN 978-1-4472-0388-9

1 3 5 7 9 8 6 4 2

A CIP catalogue record for this book is available from the British Library.

Typeset by CPI Typesetting
Printed and bound by CPI Group (UK) Ltd, Croydon, CRO 4YY

Visit **www.panmacmillan.com** to read more about all our books
and to buy them. You will also find features, author interviews and
news of any author events, and you can sign up for e-newsletters
so that you're always first to hear about our new releases.

This book is dedicated to those I've loved and lost.
And to Chandi, who makes my heart sing.

Contents

Acknowledgements

This book would not exist if it weren't for KT Forster; friend, kindred spirit, angel and my wonderful literary agent. Thank you for seeing a glimmer of potential in the original manuscript and for helping to make this dream come true. There are no words to express the extent of my gratitude.

Thanks also to Dan Waite, for introducing me to KT in the first place.

I would like to sincerely thank Ingrid Connell for allowing the dream to become reality, and her wonderful team at Macmillan, including Cindy Chan, who worked so hard editing the book. Also, thanks go to Philippa McEwan, Guy Raphael, Matt Hayes and Jon Butler for their contribution. Thanks to Mitch Robinson for the enthusiastic welcome he gave Chandi and me!

Grateful thanks to Beverley Cuddy for allowing me

to use the fabulous photographs taken by Tim Rose, and for making Chandi 'cover star' of an edition of *Dogs Today* magazine – you also made a dream come true.

Sincere thanks to my generous friend and wonderful photographer Nicky McClure for her contribution and support.

Thanks to Richard Birtles for permission to use another wonderful photograph of Chandi.

To my friends and kindred spirits, who share a similar vision, and are always there to support and encourage me; I am so thankful to have found each and every one of you. We have shared many jokes and endless amounts of 'pleasure', and long may it continue – although we may need more batteries!

In no particular order, special mentions go to Sian Davies, Tammy Shendler, Julie Newcombe, David Lamb, Janice Adler, Arlene Berman, June Jack, Darlene Stowell, Sue Powney, Bonnie Hess, Kirsty Vaughan, Loren Jensen Carter, Mandy Wheeler, Rhian Gwilt and Kayce Cover.

Roy – thank you for your friendship, and for your professional and ingenious alterations to props and for helping me cart them around. Without you, I'd still be in the car park.

To have had someone to share the whole BGT

experience was so wonderful. Debbie, I will always be so grateful for your support, friendship and all the fun we shared along the way. Thanks also to Dave for your considerable help and kindness.

Teri, Paula (Foghorn-Curtis!) and Teresa – thank you for your support and friendship and for making the journey to London to support us.

To Hannah Cole, I hope that soon you have your very own 'Chandi'. Your friendship, enthusiasm and loyalty are very precious to me.

Mum, Dad, I wish so much that you were both here to see how things turned out. I have missed sharing with you the most amazing experiences, and as a result, everything is always tinged with sadness. I hope I have made you proud. I love you both.

My beautiful girls Pepper and Chandi – without you, none of this would have been possible.

Pepper, you started this amazing journey with me and taught me so much. I love and miss you.

Chandi, you never cease to amaze me, and the love we share grows stronger by the day. Here's to many more adventures!

Anyone interested in finding out more about the training techniques described in the book or seeing some of the routines mentioned, please visit www.tinaandchandi. com.

Finally, thank you from the bottom of our hearts to everyone that voted for us on BGT, and for your continued support. It has meant more to us than you could ever imagine.

Prologue

Chandi and I stood side by side waiting to make our debut on *Britain's Got Talent*. Together we had faced every challenge life had thrown at us with unstoppable determination. Our eyes met, full of love for each other. Chandi winked; I smiled and giggled. The noise from the audience was deafening, but Chandi was totally unfazed, and unrecognizable as the frightened little pup I had met at the dog pound years before.

'Ten seconds to go,' said the assistant floor manager. Suddenly I could hear the blood pounding in my ears. 'Nine, eight, seven, six, five, four . . .'

The countdown had begun. Chandi and I were ready not just to walk out onto the stage, but to take the first step on our new adventure. It was time. The doors slid open and nothing stood in our way. Together we walked forward into the dazzling light . . .

ONE

Finding the Love of My Life

I met Pepper on 31 March 1994.

I was drawn to her straight away, despite her bedraggled appearance. She had a black shaggy coat, with a white chest, white paws and a smudge of white on her chin and above her nose. There was something about the way she sat in complete silence, despite the mayhem all around, resigned to her fate, that made me want to find out more about her.

She was in a pen at the local council dog pound with two other dogs. It didn't have a roof over it, and despite the rain, the door to the sleeping quarters was shut. The other dogs were running around the pen barking, but Pepper was sat looking at the ground. She was soaking wet, the rain running down her bowed head and dripping off her. She was very thin, quiet and seemed so sad.

My mum, Diane, had come with me to the pound that rainy Thursday afternoon to see if there was a dog I liked. About nine months earlier, just a few days before I sat my finals at Oxford University, where I read music, Mum had been diagnosed with breast cancer. It was a devastating blow. When I was much younger, Mum had endured years of ill health, suffering from crippling migraines and passing out without warning. She had spent weeks in hospital in London, but her symptoms had baffled the doctors. When I was around nine years old, the symptoms had got even worse and she developed muscle weakness in her arms and legs. They finally diagnosed her with multiple sclerosis, but we later discovered that her frightening symptoms were actually caused by severe food allergies. This revelation sparked Mum's lifelong interest in alternative therapies and organic food. By greatly adjusting her diet and lifestyle, she had improved her health and stopped the more worrying symptoms, but she was never completely well. Receiving a cancer diagnosis after everything she'd been through seemed unbearably cruel.

After seeing three of her close friends die just four years after a cancer diagnosis despite having undergone the conventional treatments of surgery, radiotherapy and chemotherapy, Mum had made the brave decision to refuse medical treatment. She was taking a holistic approach instead, using alternative therapies and dietary approaches to maintain her health for as long as possible. It was a decision I fully supported and could understand, as I shared her passion for an organic, healthy lifestyle.

Because I loved her so much, helping her through her illness had played a large part in my childhood, and now that she'd been diagnosed with cancer, I had made the decision to come home to Shropshire to be close to her after I graduated, in 1993, rather than move away to pursue a career in television. This had been my cherished ambition since the tender age of six, when I'd had the incredible experience of being on *Jim'll Fix It*. I had played the piano on the show with Jonathan Cohen, my idol from the children's programme *Play Away*.

I had started learning the piano just months before, and the violin a year later. I had begged for lessons from the age of four, and after two years Mum had realized that I was serious. I turned out to be quite talented, very keen to practise for hours on end and also blessed with perfect pitch. This means that I can name any note and recognize the key of any piece of music just by hearing it. No one knows whether you are born with perfect pitch or develop it after learning an instrument, but it is something that stays with you constantly and is hard to turn off. I can even tell you the key of a toilet flush or the hum of a light bulb!

After *Jim'll Fix It*, I took every opportunity to get involved with television again, including a second appearance on the show when I was seventeen. I once more duetted with Jonathan Cohen, but played a more advanced piece this time – the original Gershwin arrangement of 'I Got Rhythm', which Jonathan had played in the original *Fix It*. My playing had progressed massively in the intervening years: I had been awarded a scholarship at the age of eight to attend the Royal Academy of Music's Saturday junior programme, had already passed my Grade 8, with distinction, on both the piano and the violin, and had won a music scholarship to study for my A levels at Sevenoaks School, not far from where we lived at the time, in Tunbridge Wells, Kent. I appeared on the show a third time, years later, for the last ever *Jim'll Fix It*.

Living near London meant that I was able to go to the Royal Academy each Saturday, and my dad, Brian, had an easy commute to his job as an engineer at BBC Television Centre. Dad was devoted to his job, but although he provided for me, I regret that we weren't very close. Nevertheless the visits I made with him as a child to various BBC premises further fuelled my dream of working in television, and my enthusiasm for the places he adored pleased him very much. He was a quiet man with a dry sense of humour. He wasn't funny very often, but when he chose to be, and because of the rarity of it, he would have Mum and me in stitches. I loved this about him and wished that it happened more often, as it seemed to draw us all closer.

Dad took early retirement from his job and, not needing to make the commute into London any more, my parents moved to Shropshire after my A levels. Mum was desperate to get back to her roots in the Shropshire countryside, and despite the fact that I would be leaving behind all the friends I had grown up with, I fully supported her wish to move house.

Mum was my best friend. She had left her job as a nurse to be a full-time mother, and as a child I had especially loved her coming to watch me play the piano in school concerts and compete in music competitions. When we returned home, Mum and I would sit together in the kitchen, where she would have a gorgeous home-baked Victoria sponge cake waiting for us, oozing with buttercream and jam. We'd sit and eat huge wedges of the soft, fragrant sponge and she'd patiently let me talk through every single detail of the concert and relive the excitement of the evening. Even if it was a school night and it was late, Mum would let me talk and talk until I was ready to go to bed.

As a young child, I had always been happy in my own company and so preoccupied practising the piano for hours that I never wanted to mix with other children after school. If anyone knocked on the door asking if I wanted to go out to play, I would hide behind my mum's legs and whisper, 'I don't want to play. Please tell them to go away.'

Mum would politely relay the information and they soon got the message and stopped trying to include me.

When I wasn't consumed by my passion for practising the piano, I would ride my purple bicycle round and round our garden pretending it was a pony. Inspired by the touching story of a girl and her pony in a book Mum had given me, I ached for just such a relationship and, even at that young age, felt that this was what was lacking in my life. Mum was quick to change the subject whenever I begged to learn to horse ride, and instead continued to encourage me with my schoolwork and musical endeavours. We simply couldn't afford riding lessons on top of my music lessons.

Mum had also been obsessed with horses when she was young. Her parents didn't have money for such an expensive pursuit either, so, undeterred, she started working at the local riding stables in Ludlow, and eventually, much to her delight, the owner taught her to ride in exchange for the work she did around the stables. When she could ride well enough and the horses weren't booked for lessons, Mum and a couple of horse-mad friends would be allowed to take them out for the day. The stories she told me about how they would ride up to the woods and then sit on the ground sharing their lunch, the horses around them, sounded so good to me.

Mum was a petite five feet two inches tall, a size that belied her strength. Her long hair was beautiful, thick and shiny, and she was a bit of a daredevil. Just for fun, she would persuade her friends to ride the horses back to the stables sitting on them facing the wrong way. They would ride like that through Ludlow town, hooves clattering on the cobbles and people stopping to point and stare as they rode past.

Mum left school as soon as she could and went to work full time at the stables. The owner had become ill and Mum was put in charge of the whole place and loved it. Thinking of her future, she applied for a job as a groom at a showjumping yard and left home at sixteen to pursue her career. After just a few short months, though, she realized that she wasn't content being a groom; she wanted to be a showjumper. Unfortunately there was no hope of that ever happening, not because she didn't have the potential, but simply because she didn't have the financial means. She made the decision to leave and forget all about her dream as she knew it would never come true. She enrolled as a student nurse and it was many years before she rode a horse again.

I imagine that's why she was always so quick to discourage me when I asked for riding lessons as a child. Instead I was encouraged to keep up with my music practice and schoolwork, as Mum knew from her own experience that without fistfuls of money, horse riding was not going to lead anywhere.

When I was nine, I made friends with a black and white Border collie named Chloe in a garden backing onto my school playing field. I would sit and stroke her during break times and she became my imaginary friend when I wasn't with her. Chloe was with me in spirit all the time, even during a family holiday to Bournemouth; I let her share my seat in the back of our camper van. Finally Mum realized something wasn't quite right and asked why I only sat on half of my seat. Up until that point I hadn't told her about Chloe and how attached I had become to this gentle soul who whimpered so pitifully when I had to leave her. But now, questioned directly, I blurted everything out, much to Mum's surprise.

Having longed for a pony herself as a child, and adored her own childhood dog, Mum understood completely, and three years later, she took me to choose a yellow Labrador from a wriggly litter of fat four-week-old puppies. I was in heaven! We named him Chandie and brought him home two weeks later. I loved everything about him. When he was old enough, I taught him to negotiate jumps and other obstacles built from flowerpots and broomsticks I found in the garden shed. We would spend hours racing round these makeshift courses, having so much fun, and Chandie was a very willing participant.

Chandie was the family dog, but as Mum was with him most of the time, he was really her dog. I looked forward to the day when I had my own dog, and most of all, I still longed for that unconditional love I had decided years before that only an animal could truly offer.

After graduating in music at Oxford, and still in shock over Mum's recent cancer diagnosis, I started teaching the piano and violin in a local school two mornings a week, and privately from my parents' house, where I was living. Teaching was never what I wanted to do, but it allowed me to stay in Shropshire to be near Mum.

Now that I was earning my own living, and after much discussion, the moment I had been waiting for was finally here: I was going to have my own dog. That rainy day, Mum drove me to the local council dog pound and we went through the metal gate to the kennels and saw pen after pen full of dogs of all shapes and sizes. The noise was deafening and it was difficult to concentrate, but one bedraggled dog caught my eye straight away.

I crouched down next to the bars and said hello to her. To start with, she didn't take any notice, but I just kept talking. I wanted to see if she would respond to me.

Finally she raised her head, blinking her deep brown eyes as she focused on my face. I smiled, bringing my hand up in front of the bars so she could sniff my fingers. Despite the sign warning about sticking your fingers through the bars of the pens, I reached through and gently stroked the end of her nose. She pushed the side of her face against the bars so I could stroke her cheek and the top of her head. All the while I was talking gently to her as we looked at each other. I knew that this dog was supposed to be with me. Pepper didn't have a name then, only a number.

Nothing much was known about Pepper's history. All we knew was that she had been spotted as a stray wandering around on the army camp near Telford, scavenging for food. The dog warden had been sent to catch her and that's how she'd ended up in the pound. I've no idea how long she had been living rough, but she was covered in cuts and bruises, and her ribs were like a toast rack.

I wasn't sure Mum was going to let me adopt this long-haired dog I'd fallen for, but to my delight, she gave her consent. She knew how lonely I was without any of my school or university friends nearby, and I think letting me have my own dog in the house was her way of thanking me for supporting her by moving back to Shropshire.

I left a deposit with the pound to reserve her and had to wait an agonizing six days before I could take her home. She had only been at the pound for a day, so could in theory still be claimed by her owner, if she had one. I was so glad when no one came, and when we returned the following week, I was allowed to take her home. On 6 April 1994, Pepper became mine.

After a week of being cold and wet, she was in an even sorrier state when I arrived with Mum to collect her. She was desperately thin, absolutely stank to high heaven and had a bone-shattering cough: she had been infected with kennel cough while at the pound and was quite poorly.

I picked her up and placed her in the back of the car on an old blanket. She was very light and didn't struggle. Mum drove so I could spend the journey home leaning round into the back of the car and gently stroking Pepper's head as she lay still and quiet. We were almost there when Pepper's body began to heave and she vomited. She looked up at me, stretching her neck and swallowing hard to try to get rid of the acid in her throat. I felt so sorry for her and thought how wretched she must feel. A warm bath, a meal and a soft bed would make her feel better, and she didn't have long to wait before her new life could well and truly begin.

Our new home in Shropshire, Orchard House, was much nicer than where we had lived in Kent. It had a large garden that wrapped round the house and was filled with flowers. In Tunbridge Wells, Dad used to have to check daily for used needles thrown into our garden by the drug addicts who congregated by our garage. Now we had a beautiful view over open fields to the rear and I loved hanging out of my bedroom window on summer evenings and watching the sun set. It was very relaxing and peaceful, with the only noise coming from the wood pigeons, which would coo loudly.

It was obvious that Pepper had been very badly treated wherever she had lived before as she would cower if I picked anything up near her, and would frequently wet the floor in fear. She was destructive if left alone for even a few minutes. All of this was challenging to deal with, and not really what I was expecting. I was quite naive at that time about exactly how much someone can screw up a dog through ignorance of the level of care and training a dog needs, particularly when young.

We had got Chandie as a six-week-old puppy. He had never suffered any trauma and learned how to behave right from the start. I realized pretty soon that having a dog is like having a child. They both need parenting that is fair and consistent. Dogs are extremely intelligent creatures that need constant guidance right from the start, otherwise they can develop problem behaviour. Once they reach adolescence, at around nine months old, and have lost their cute puppy appeal, many dogs get thrown out and dumped. Pepper was one such dog – the people at the pound thought she was between eight and ten months when I rescued her. I was determined to help Pepper overcome the effects of her early life. She was *my* dog now, and in helping her, I would learn a great deal about myself and the kind of person I wanted to be.

Every morning I would get up early, go downstairs and walk into the utility room where Pepper slept. On opening the door, Pepper would be cowering in her bed, which she would instantly wet. To start with, I didn't have much of a clue how to cope with her; going to her and stroking her while she was in her bed didn't seem to be helping. No matter how unthreatening I tried to be, I was met with the same reaction every morning.

It was time for a different approach. I needed to make our first meeting of the day less stressful for Pepper and make her anticipate good things when she saw me in the morning. I came up with a simple idea: instead of going into the utility room to greet Pepper, I would open the front door, quietly push the utility-room door open, then quickly creep outside and call Pepper out to me.

The first morning I did this, I watched from outside as, a little hesitantly, Pepper's nose appeared around the door when I called her. As soon as I saw her start to come out, I began to call her more enthusiastically, making my voice as animated and exciting as possible. When Pepper realized where I was and started to approach me, I began to run around outside, continuing to call her and encourage her to come over to me.

She couldn't resist finding out what on earth I was up to and joining in my game of just running around for the sheer sake of running around! Once I got Pepper involved in the game, running with me and jumping up in excitement as we ran, it was time to actually say good morning and hello to her, so I stopped running and bent down to stroke her.

She leaned into my legs and then jumped up, planting her front paws almost on my shoulders. I had started to spot the signs when she was getting ready to launch herself on me and was quick to move away so she wasn't successful. After her attempt failed, I began to run around again. Pepper soon realized that I didn't want her to jump on me and that the fun happened when all her four paws were on the ground.

This was definitely a better start to the day than seeing Pepper cowering in her bed and so I continued with this new approach for the next couple of days. On the third day, as I was coming down the stairs, I heard Pepper get up from her bed and snort and snuffle at the crack under the door. She was ready for the fun to start, and with the front door open, I pushed the utility-room door open, turned and ran outside.

On the fourth morning, I decided that I would go

into the utility room and see what her reaction would be. I held my breath as I stood outside the door, but I could hear Pepper was already up and her claws were doing a kind of tap dance on the lino as she waited in anticipation of being let out. I pushed the door open a little and walked in. Pepper wagged her tail when she saw me and started leaning on me for a fuss. That was the first morning we went through the front door side by side. My plan had worked: I had managed to replace the negative associations Pepper had from her previous home with happy, positive ones. She knew she was safe with me.

I didn't think too much about why Pepper had been so scared when the door opened after she had been on her own all night, but surely someone had done something to her to make her react like that. It was my job to fix my broken, shaggy dog and build her confidence. I was determined to be the person who didn't let her down and to show her that she really could trust me. I was pleased with the start I'd made, but I wanted to do more for her.

Even though Mum had agreed to let me have Pepper at home, for most of the time she had to stay in the utility room. Chandie was allowed in the kitchen and the living room in the evenings; Pepper wasn't. Mum was particularly worried about the carpets getting ruined. For now, anyway, she sadly decided that two dogs loose in the house was too much.

Whenever I left Pepper on her own in the utility room, I would never know what I was going to find when I came back. Her separation anxiety manifested itself in copious chewing, which seemed to start the moment I left the room. She would chew huge holes in the large towels that covered her bed and leave her bedding soaking wet. Pepper progressed from this to chewing on my favourite pair of boots, and after that she decided that the skirting board needed some alteration and managed to rip part of it off the wall. That day, I returned to find splinters of wood all over her bed and not a whole lot of the skirting board left. Mum was cross, but Dad said it didn't matter and replaced it a few days later. In the meantime, Pepper took something of a dislike to the doormat that sat by the back door and managed to rip it into a million tiny pieces in a very short space of time.

When I wasn't teaching, Pepper and I would be outside together, whatever the weather. I would make sure that she was tired out before I went to work so she would sleep in her bed and not miss me while I was gone (or chew anything else). I didn't like to think of her on her own, but I had to work and knowing that she was fast asleep meant I could relax.

In the warmer months, Mum would let her out in the garden and one day, when I arrived home after a tiring morning of teaching, Mum confessed over lunch that they had lost Pepper for a while. Dad had finally spotted her outside the gate at the front of the house, sat patiently waiting to be let in. They had no idea where she had been. This became a regular adventure for Pepper when I wasn't there. It wasn't until we blocked up every gap in the garden that her mini-excursions came to an end.

Pepper still managed to have fun in the garden, though. One day in May, about six weeks after she came to live with us, I was in the kitchen with Mum, preparing some food, while Pepper busied herself outside. When I looked through the window, I saw her chasing her tail, spinning round and round, and getting increasingly frustrated. Pepper stopped and sat down in a huff, then noticed that her tail was now within reach! She lunged and grabbed it. She was so thrilled that she didn't let go, which meant she had to spiral towards the house when I called her in for food. Mum and I were in fits of laughter, and when Pepper got to the door, she fell over with dizziness and finally let her tail go, lying spreadeagled on the floor until the room stopped spinning. Pepper's newfound zest for life was very different to the sad and confused dog I'd brought home just weeks earlier, and it was wonderful to see her happy.

Eventually Mum allowed Pepper into the kitchen when I was there and she would lie next to Chandie on the mat by the door and rest her head on his back. Chandie didn't seem to mind having Pepper around, but he didn't want to play with her much. By this time he was nine years old and seemed to be slowing down. Unbeknown to us at that point, Chandie had liver cancer and would very sadly die just eight months after we brought Pepper home.

To build Pepper's confidence further, common sense told me that training her was the only thing to do, so I set about teaching her basic commands like how to sit, lie down and come when called. She was very intelligent and eager to learn and picked up these things quickly.

I was keen to take Pepper to a dog show to see how her training was progressing. I had enjoyed competing in music competitions when I was younger and part of me missed the excitement and preparation. Here was something Pepper and I could do together that offered a new challenge and gave us both something to aim for.

The first dog show we went to took place a few months after Pepper entered my life. As Mum, Pepper and I made our way around the showground, which was heaving with dogs and people, I couldn't help but feel a little excited by the atmosphere and seeing other dogs, most of which were behaving impeccably, in action in the various classes. I had never been to a dog show before, but I knew, after just being there for a few minutes, that this was going to be the first of many for us.

Pepper was incredibly excited about being surrounded by so many other dogs – I hadn't anticipated exactly how much – and she seemed to forget everything that I had taught her, yanking my arm out of its socket as she pulled in every direction on her lead. I was disappointed at how she was behaving and realized we had a great deal of work still to do. Being a novice dog trainer, I hadn't appreciated that I needed to train Pepper in many different locations and with increasing levels of distraction. She had been performing perfectly in the privacy of our garden at home and when we were together out on our walks, but with so many dogs all around to distract her, I had really thrown her in at the deep end and it wasn't surprising that she was overwhelmed.

I left Pepper with Mum for a few minutes while I went off to find the loo. While I was washing my hands, I heard this awful wailing noise. I had no idea what it was, but when I returned and saw Mum and Pepper in the crowd, I realized that the noise was coming from my beloved dog! Mum told me she had never been so embarrassed in her life; Pepper had started to howl as soon as she had lost sight of me.

I was mortified to see that we were getting some very

dirty looks from the handlers working with their dogs in the ring closest to us and I realized later that this was one of the rings where the obedience competitions were taking place. Pepper was proving to be excellent distraction training for the other dogs.

We didn't have a great time at the show and we left early. Pepper had pulled me all over the place and I was absolutely exhausted. I was sad and a little disappointed that Pepper hadn't behaved as well as I knew she could, but seeing some of the other dogs competing in the obedience classes just made me more determined to succeed with Pepper. I'd also taken a bit of a shine to the colourful rosettes that were being handed out to the winners of each class, and the way people were displaying them so proudly in their cars. I rather liked the idea of doing that myself, but I couldn't help feeling just then that a car full of rosettes was a very long way off.

I decided to try training Pepper for agility competitions, which is like showjumping for dogs, and after the disaster of the recent dog show, we enrolled in our local agility class, hoping to get some help from the trainers there. Pepper was a natural at the equipment, mastering all of it in a short space of time, but we had one huge problem – her lack of early socialization with dogs meant that she was so distracted and fearful of the other dogs around her that she couldn't concentrate. Despite my best efforts, she would charge over aggressively to any dog she took a dislike to and wouldn't come back when I called her. We persevered for a few more months but with no great improvement, so we left and didn't return. Agility, it seemed, wasn't for us, but I certainly wasn't going to give up on Pepper.

Training a dog was all new to me and I was learning as much as Pepper. My initial attempts at training her involved telling her off when she did something wrong, and I'm ashamed to say that I did, on more than one occasion, smack her. I justified this by reminding myself that this was my experience when I was growing up – when I was naughty, I would get a telling-off, usually accompanied by a smacked bottom – and we are all a product of our experiences. I soon realized that it was *my* choice how I reacted to Pepper's behaviour; she was my responsibility and I decided I owed it to her to find a better way and not just repeat a pattern that had been passed down the generations.

I confess it did take me many months to retrain myself not to react to bad behaviour in such a way and I just hated myself after I'd shouted at Pepper and saw the crestfallen look on her face. I decided to praise her so much more than I had been doing for whatever she did well and for any effort she put into doing the correct thing. I made it my mission to make Pepper feel like the cleverest dog in the entire world whenever she performed the simplest task I asked. I would cheer and clap and go on and on about how wonderful she was. I didn't stop praising her and acting like a bit of a lunatic until she was all smiles and wiggles and running around exuberantly.

This new approach began having the desired effect and Pepper keenly responded to everything I asked as long as there weren't any other dogs around to distract her. I could clearly see that she was trying her hardest.

It was difficult for me to stop saying, 'No,' when she did the wrong thing, but I eventually managed it and decided that to further encourage her, I would acknowledge her efforts by putting a name to whatever she had just done. I was formulating my own training system based on encouragement and support, and we were both making amazing progress adjusting our behaviour. I was learning how to get the best out of Pepper by building her confidence and celebrating all her achievements, no matter how small they may have seemed. It was my responsibility not to be just another person who let Pepper down. Her destiny, and indeed my own, was very much in my hands.

Watching Pepper's reactions, I realized that it was her nature, and indeed the nature of most dogs, to be forgiving of what can only be described as my initially disrespectful behaviour towards her. Even if I hadn't been completely intent on becoming a better human being and had continued to tell her off, she would forgive me every time and still love me. That was not good enough for me, though; I needed to deserve her growing love and trust, not have it in spite of my failings.

Those early months and years with Pepper, we learned together, and I was gradually becoming as trustworthy and dependable as she was. It became vitally important to continue to congratulate Pepper for her achievements as I watched her begin to grow and blossom into a dog that oozed confidence and personality in every situation.

We had started to work on some classic dog tricks like shaking paws, sitting up and begging, and rolling over, but instead of being content with basic tricks, I was always looking for a way to extend the trick a little further, making it more difficult, interesting and impressive. A simple shake of a paw, for example, could be turned into marching on the spot. All I had to do was teach Pepper to lift both front paws and then practise lifting them alternately. To make it even better, we practised until Pepper would lift either foot on a verbal command alone. This made for a much neater trick without me having to hold my hands out for her to touch with her paws.

I constantly talked to her when we went out for walks.

A walk for us was an adventure, not just necessary exercise for Pepper. I would try to experience what she was experiencing on whatever level I could: I would look down into the rabbit holes and at the tree roots that she was keen to explore. After a while, when Pepper found something that was interesting to her, she would stop what she was doing, raise her head and look over at me. From the expression on her face, I soon got the message that she wanted me to come and have a look too.

We were lucky where we lived, as there was a footpath at the top of our cul-de-sac that led onto miles of footpaths over fields and through woods. There were so many paths to explore and we would take a different one every day. I loved being out with Pepper, just the two of us, enjoying each other's company and the wonderful ever-changing scenery around us. She adored being in water and there were many shallow streams for her to lie in. As she lay in the cold water, her long fur would float around her like the skirt of a hovercraft. When she stood up, she would look pretty comical, as the wet fur on her legs would be plastered down, making her look like a cartoon dog with tiny stick legs and a big hairy body. I later discovered she loved to swim too.

When it was really hot, we would go to Carding Mill Valley in Church Stretton, where there were three pools of water that used to form part of a reservoir. Pepper would bark for me to throw a ball in as far as I could and without hesitation she would wade into the water and swim furiously after it to bring it back. She would do this for hours, loving every minute.

Spending time with Pepper was the best thing in the whole world for me and I just adored my gorgeous dog, whether I was grooming her, walking with her or simply clearing up after her. I was learning about Pepper all the time. I was watching her body language and facial expressions in response to different situations. Her ears and eyes held major clues to how she was feeling and I learned to read them all. She could hold her ears in many different positions and, coupled with the expression in her eyes, I realized she was constantly communicating with me. Her ears were big and floppy, and the fur on them was slightly wavy. When she was sad, she would flatten them right back, and if I'd just reprimanded her for something, she would also put her head down. To add to the effect, she would simultaneously gaze up at me with her beautiful nut-brown eyes from under her long eyelashes. She had the same look as Princess Diana during the famous *Panorama* interview. It was impossible to be cross with Pepper when she was looking at me in such a sorrowful and completely charming way, and she knew it.

The more attached I grew to Pepper and the more I

came to understand her, the more my opinion of animals in general began to change. I realized that although Pepper couldn't verbalize her thoughts, she was certainly capable of communicating. I really came to feel that I understood her and we were growing very close.

It was around this time that I decided that I had to become a vegetarian. If my dog was so intelligent and displayed such a huge range of emotions, surely other animals must have the same capacity. The more I thought about the way animals are treated the world over, the more upset I became. Refusing to eat meat was the first thing that I could do. The second thing was ensuring that I wasn't a hypocrite, so I began feeding Pepper on organic, free range meat, reared to the highest standards, not only for the welfare of the animals, but also for Pepper's health. I didn't want to feed her on meat that was laced with antibiotics, hormones and genetically modified grains.

Something else happened that made my decision to stop eating meat easier. One morning, Pepper and I went walking through a field behind our house in which some cows were grazing in the far corner. Not wanting to disturb them, Pepper and I gave them a very wide berth. We had almost got to the stile when I heard heavy footsteps behind me. I turned to see a very large black and white cow stood a few feet away looking straight at me.

I was a little frightened at that point, as I had no idea what this huge animal was thinking. I grabbed Pepper just as she was about to wander over to the cow; I was frightened she might be kicked, or worse. I was nervous about turning my back on the cow and making a dash for the stile, so instead, having given the situation a few seconds' thought, I held my hand out to it. As soon as I stretched out my hand, the cow stepped forward and Pepper started to bark. The cow was startled, and so was I. After asking Pepper to stop and reassuring her, while keeping a firm hold of her collar, I once again stretched my hand out towards the cow. This time, she stepped forward and put her big nose directly in my hand. I was so surprised: we both just stood there looking at one another. I moved my hand and stroked her neck, and to my surprise the cow started to behave a bit like a huge dog, trying to get closer to me, wanting some attention. A little stunned by the experience, we didn't stay for long.

The next day, walking through the same field, this cow once again left her herd to come over to us, and I stopped and stroked her and talked to her. In fact she grew so used to me that when the herd was grazing in the field behind our garden, she would stop and look round if I called to her from my bedroom window.

After this unexpected friendship, there was no way I could ever eat meat again, I simply couldn't, and more than that I decided there and then that every animal that entered my life in any capacity would always be treated with the greatest of respect. I threw out all the cosmetics, shampoo and anything that I suspected had been tested on animals and replaced them with cruelty-free, organic versions. Two months later, the cows were taken from the field, and most likely sent for slaughter. It made me feel physically sick to think about it.

After realizing that dog agility would never be Pepper's strong suit, I decided to have a go at some more obedience training. For Christmas my dad gave me a book I'd been wanting on competitive obedience training and I set about teaching Pepper every exercise, from scent work to distance control. She picked everything up really quickly.

The exercise that I loved most, though, was heelwork. Pepper would walk on my left side and would have to keep her right shoulder close to my left leg as we walked and turned in different directions. We would work on perfecting this heelwork for many, many hours and Pepper soon learned that she had to keep a constant position and not let her body swing wide or bump into my leg. This meant that she had to concentrate very hard and watch me closely all the time, and it turned out to be something she loved as much as I did.

I had also started working with Pepper at the local

park where there were lots of dogs, and as long as Pepper was engaged with me and concentrating on her heel-work, she completely ignored every distraction as she trotted stylishly by my side, gazing up at me. Having never trained a dog before, I really had no idea whether we were doing it correctly. The obedience book was very helpful, but the time had come to see if all this further training was paying off.

With great excitement and a certain amount of trepidation, I scoured the advertisements in *Dog World* newspaper for an exemption dog show that wasn't too far away. Exemption shows, or companion dog shows as they are now known, are informal events licensed by the Kennel Club, the main dog-training and welfare body in the UK. I found a show at the National Canine Defence League, now called Dogs Trust, in Evesham, that had obedience competitions, and Pepper and I stepped up our training in the two weeks before the competition. By this point, Pepper and I had been together for just eleven months and I couldn't believe how far we'd both come.

Show day arrived and I drove to the show with Pepper groomed and looking stunningly gorgeous in her bright red collar and lead. Mum didn't come with us this time and I was feeling a little anxious in spite of all the training we had done, as I couldn't help but remember what a disaster the first show had been, and wonder if this was going to be a repeat.

We were eligible for two obedience classes: the very first class, for dogs new to obedience and then also the second class, which was for dogs that had never won an obedience class. There were just over a hundred people entered in the first class, which seemed a ridiculously large number, and I felt sure we didn't stand a chance. I didn't even know how Pepper was going to behave at that point, as I had left her to wait in the car while I went off to enter her for the classes.

When I returned to the car, Pepper was sat bolt upright looking through the window. Her ears were up and she seemed excited. I opened the door and she waited patiently until I had attached her lead to her collar and then jumped out and stood still, without me asking, and waited while I locked the car. I was half expecting her to leap from the car and then just tow me over to where all the other dogs were, as she had done at the last show. I praised her for standing still and waiting so beautifully and then we walked side by side over to where the obedience classes were taking place.

Pepper's behaviour was absolutely perfect. She was a model of composure and self-control, and I felt on top of the world. We found a space by one of the rings and sat down together on the grass to watch some of the other competitors with their dogs in the ring. I was excited to see that what I was doing with Pepper at home looked similar to what they were doing with their dogs and I felt a wave of relief. Our turn soon came and Pepper focused all her attention on me as we walked across to the ring to compete in our very first obedience competition.

We went into the ring and followed the directions the steward gave us: walk forward; halt; walk forward; left turn; left about turn; right turn; halt. Pepper was really paying attention and I was so pleased with her. We had certainly made progress over the last few months, as Pepper was unrecognizable as the lunatic dog from the last show!

When all the other competitors had done their turn in the ring, it was time to do the stays. This is where everyone in the class first has to ask their dog to stay in a sit position for a minute or so and then ask for them to stay lying down for slightly longer. For each of the stay exercises, you had to walk away from your dog and you weren't allowed to speak to your dog.

Pepper remained still as a rock in the stays for the first class, but when it came to the stays for the second class, I made the mistake of facing her while she was doing the exercises, which wasn't how we practised it at home. We'd always done the stays with my back to her, but the steward gave us the choice of facing our dogs or turning away from them and I chose poorly. A few seconds into the sit stay, Pepper got up, walked towards me and positioned herself right in front of me. This was entirely my fault, but it taught me a valuable lesson.

The winners were to be announced shortly after the end of the stays, just as soon as the points had been added up and the final marks awarded. I sat with Pepper on the grass, running my fingers through her glossy, wavy coat, and wondered why we were bothering to wait with so many other competitors in the same class. When the judges and stewards came back into the ring, they started calling a list of competitor numbers, and surprisingly we were among them.

The placings for the first class were called in reverse order out of the handlers and dogs who had just been called back into the ring. The prizes were given out to the sixth-place dog and handler, then the fifth. Once the second-place team had been called into the centre of the ring to receive their rosette, I realized that, unless a serious mistake had been made, Pepper and I had won the class! It seemed like an age before this was confirmed. I was expecting to be told that a mistake had been made and that we shouldn't be in the ring at all. I held my breath as the announcement was made and forgot to move forward as our number was called. It wasn't until I noticed the steward urgently gesturing for me to come forward and receive our rosette that I realized we had actually won!

The judge shook me by the hand and told me that Pepper had won without losing any points, which meant that she had done everything perfectly. I couldn't believe what I was hearing, nor could I believe that I had managed to achieve all this by using a book to train her. The judge then told me not to be disappointed about the next class and whispered in my ear that if Pepper had done the stays perfectly, as she had done in this first class, we would have won that too, as we were in the lead going into the stays. As a result, we weren't even placed in the second class, but I was grateful that the judge had told me why.

I felt so proud of my beautiful Pepper and everything we had achieved together. In just eleven short months, I had managed to completely turn around Pepper's behaviour. She had blossomed into a beautiful, confident dog, such a far cry from the first time I met her, pitifully thin, soaking wet and miserable. I was so in love with her, and from the way she was gazing up at me, I knew the feeling was mutual.

Pepper and I were definitely on the right track and I was keen to find some more shows to enter, to see if we could repeat our success. We drove home that day with the beautiful red rosette proudly pinned to the passenger sun visor for all to see. When I didn't have to use my left hand to change gear, I held Pepper's paw. I was so proud of her.

That summer, and for four years after, we entered every exemption show we could find and travelled miles each weekend in our very old but reliable red Volvo. We would enter each of the obedience classes for which we were eligible and would win them all at each show. We started entering the showing classes too, as Pepper was stunningly beautiful, and we would win most of the ones we entered and, more often than not, 'Best in Show' as well! We would come home laden with rosettes and trophies, proud mementos of our time together and Pepper's brilliant performance.

Pepper and I would work hard during the week to keep improving further and I relished the challenge of teaching her more demanding and complicated exercises for every class. She retained her cheeky streak outside of the shows, though, and Mum used to complain about Pepper's wayward behaviour and attitude to being told off: if Pepper ever did something naughty, she would pretend to be sorry while Mum told her off, adopting her customary sorrowful expression, with her head down, the whites of her eyes showing underneath her beautiful brown irises. She would wait until Mum had finished being cross with her, then run behind and practically lift Mum off the floor with her nose! Much to Mum's annoyance, Pepper even knew that she had to run and dodge Mum's hand as she flapped it round to stop her. Pepper would then charge off, mouth hanging open, tongue lolling out, delighted with herself. I always promised to have a word with Pepper, but it never had any effect! The only person Pepper ever responded to was me. She wouldn't even sit if someone else told her to – it was as though she couldn't hear them.

Being with Pepper was all I wanted and I was completely happy being in her company. I had found a truly loyal, devoted friend and it was a special feeling to be loved and to have someone to love. I constantly tried to be the friend to her that she was to me.

In 1998, I heard about Heelwork to Music. There was a competition being held by Rugby Dog Training Club, in Ryton-on-Dunsmore, near Coventry. The idea of combining my love of music with my passion for dog training really appealed to me and I decided that this was going to be our new challenge. We could build on all the obedience heelwork we had been working on and incorporate the large repertoire of tricks Pepper had mastered to create a routine set to the music of our choice.

Being fascinated with horses when I was younger,

one year, when I was almost fifteen, my parents had taken me to the horse show held at Olympia just before Christmas. It was at that show that I saw dog agility for the first time. I also saw an impressive dressage display in which the horse was actually skipping. I researched this movement when I got home, as it was just the most fascinatingly beautiful thing I'd ever seen an animal do. The movement is officially called one tempis but as you watch, the horse is actually hopping on each front leg in turn and truly is skipping.

A year before hearing about the Heelwork to Music competition, I remembered this movement and wondered if it would be possible to teach Pepper to do it, just as a fun exercise. Having a leg at each corner, it was, in theory, possible. Nevertheless, training a horse to do one tempis takes years and it is an extremely advanced dressage movement. I needed to figure out how to teach Pepper, as I knew that it would be very eye-catching and was something I'd never seen a dog do before. I didn't worry about teaching her the movement, though, as I didn't really think that we'd ever actually master it; it was just something else for us to try.

Breaking the movement down into component parts, I taught Pepper to lift each front leg in turn on command. That was the easy bit. The hard bit was to get her to understand that she needed to hop on the front leg that wasn't lifted high in the air. It took me months of bending down and getting Pepper to touch my hand with her front paw, encouraging her to put in a little hop in order to be able to reach my hand.

Slowly but surely we were getting closer to the movement, and then one day everything just seemed to click into place in Pepper's head and she skipped along with me! I went absolutely nuts praising her and we both ended up in a heap on the ground, with Pepper licking me and me hugging her. We'd mastered it and Pepper had realized that she always had to adjust the length of her stride to match mine so our steps were identical. We were becoming a formidable team and there were new challenges on the horizon.

We had continued to enter the obedience shows and now had a large collection of trophies and rosettes, which I proudly displayed on top of the bookcase in my bedroom, but I knew that Pepper was finding the exercises really easy to perform and was capable of much more. We definitely needed to take things to the next level. The Heelwork to Music competition would do exactly that and, with this new move, was to change our path for ever.

Being a new discipline, Heelwork to Music wasn't yet a Kennel Club-recognized sport, and in fact wasn't to become recognized until 2003, with an official competition being held at Crufts in 2005, but we were extremely excited to be participating in this demonstration event. In order to compete in such a large show, though, Pepper had to be registered with the Kennel Club. Growing up, I had decided that any dog of mine would have the prefix 'Bluecroft' to their name, so I registered Pepper with the name Bluecroft Love of My Life because she really *was* the love of my life.

I chose a piece of music that was the correct length of four minutes – 'Song of the Bells' by Leroy Anderson – and choreographed a routine. I carried our tape recorder up into the fields behind our house and, with various rocks and stones, marked the outline of a ring to the size specified on the show schedule. We practised our routine complete with music for weeks, and when it came to the day before the show, I was terrified. I didn't sleep much that night, and by the time we got to Coventry and parked the car at the show venue, I was feeling sick with nerves.

I had to wait nearly all day until it was our turn in the ring, which only heightened my anxiety, but as I was warming Pepper up to perform our routine, I suddenly felt a little more confident as Pepper looked up at me with keenness written all over her face.

Our names were announced: '. . . and into the ring now please welcome Tina Humphrey and Bluecroft Love of My Life.'

We walked to our starting position and nodded for the

music to start. We went through all our moves, including the much practised one tempis, as well as I could have hoped for, considering my nerves and it being Pepper's first time in such a huge hall with so many people watching.

We took a bow side by side to lots of applause from the audience, and Pepper and I bounced out of the ring. I could see from the way she was throwing her head around that she was excited and had truly enjoyed herself. I was so glad that we had plucked up the courage to have a go.

When our scores were announced after our turn, we were in the lead. I couldn't believe it – it was our first Heelwork to Music show. There were still more competitors to have their turn in the ring, and two of them were handlers who had done well with their dogs in the competition in previous years. By the end of the show, we had dropped a couple of places, but I was overwhelmed and absolutely delighted to be placed third.

Being placed in the top five of this national competition meant an automatic invite to perform at Earls Court in London at the Kennel Club's Discover Dogs later that year. Exhilarated, we made the journey home. I couldn't wait for that day to come. Before it did, though, I was to visit the dog pound once more.

*

With Pepper and me so happy in our life together, I began to think about finding another dog to train and be a friend for her. Of course, living in my parents' home, it wasn't up to me, and Mum made it very clear that if I wanted another dog, I would have to move out.

That was easier said than done, as property was so expensive, and I had Pepper to consider as well. Nevertheless, one day, I saw a tiny flat advertised for sale that I could afford, and best of all, it was in Church Stretton, just a few miles from my parents' house. Pepper and I loved Church Stretton and its miles of open moorland, valleys and streams, the Long Mynd, which provided us with many interesting adventures together. I made an appointment to view the tiny studio flat, taking Mum and Pepper with me, of course, and I felt very excited as we drove up the beautiful tree-lined no-through road, where a big house that had been converted into eight studio flats was situated.

At the end of the road, just a few hundred yards from the property, was a footpath that led down through a wood and out onto one of our favourite walks. I felt at home right away and was anxious for the estate agent to arrive to show us round. When he finally arrived, apologizing for being late, we all walked up the two flights of stairs around to the back of the building, where number 7 had its own entrance. As the flat was unoccupied, the agent had agreed that Pepper could come in too and I was delighted. Pepper was also excited to take a look inside, but was being very well behaved.

The instant I walked through the front door into the flat, I loved it. It was perfect for me and Pepper. It had a small kitchen with room for everything we needed, a bathroom and one large main room that was a living room and bedroom combined. It also had a small entrance hall and three large walk-in cupboards. The icing on the cake had to be the small balcony, which was accessed via a door from the main room. Half the balcony belonged to this flat, and half to the flat next door. It turned out that the owners of the flat next door lived in London and only visited occasionally, and they were happy for me to use the whole balcony and put plants out there as well. Pepper clearly shared my enthusiasm for the flat. She suddenly tugged her lead out of my hand, ran over to the large bay window in the main room and, jumping up, placed her front paws on the window-sill and looked out, turning her head quickly from side to side and taking everything in. When she had finished at that window, she ran into the kitchen and examined the view from there. Once she had seen enough, she ran back to where my mum, the agent and I were all standing in amazement watching her actions. She then gave an excited squeak, licked my hand and plonked herself down directly in front of me with her mouth hanging open in a huge grin. I took that to mean the flat had Pepper's seal of approval. What more did I need?

Having my own place meant that I could now make my own rules about how I wanted to live and where Pepper was allowed. Living in my parents' house, I had always tried to be respectful of their wishes, so I relished my new freedom. The first thing I did when Pepper and I finally moved in was to place her bed right next to mine. If she wanted to, she was allowed to sleep on my bed with me.

Pepper loved to lie on the far end of the balcony and watch the world go by, and I would often go and sit with her. It was very peaceful, with only trees in front of us, and the occasional glimpse of hills in the distance when the wind gently moved the branches.

We both loved having our own home. I wasn't far from my parents' house, and was there four afternoons and evenings a week because I was still running my teaching business from their house as my new flat wasn't big enough for a piano.

Now five years on from her diagnosis, Mum was still in good health, so clearly her use of alternative therapies and healthy lifestyle were keeping the cancer at bay. She had supported my decision to move out by giving me the deposit, which meant that I could afford the mortgage.

Everything seemed to be going well, and looking at her, it was hard to believe that there was a ticking cancer time bomb slowly growing inside her. Nevertheless, I was glad that moving out didn't mean that I had to move far.

Two

Pink-nosed Puppy

The first time I met Chandi was on the afternoon of 11 November 1998. I wanted to give another unwanted dog a chance at a good and interesting life, so I visited the same dog pound that had given me my beautiful Pepper – I didn't consider for even a second buying a puppy from a breeder. I expected to have to visit the kennels many times before finding another dog destined to be mine, but destiny was to play its part on my very first visit.

I walked down the rows of pens with their metal gates, gazing at the sad faces of the dogs. Some of them barked aggressively as you looked at them, while others would just sit motionless, each with their own sad tale to tell. Reaching the end of the row of pens and not seeing a dog that caught my eye, I turned round and, with my head down, quickly retraced my steps. I couldn't look at the dogs on the way back. I felt guilty that I could escape and they were trapped, just waiting for someone to give them a chance in life.

A few of the dogs I recognized as having been there when I adopted Pepper from the pound four years earlier, and even now my eyes fill with tears when I think about the life that they, and others like them, have. Some might say that they are the lucky ones – this pound doesn't destroy dogs, but many up and down the country do. Shockingly, around 150 dogs are destroyed every week in local-authority pounds because no one wants them.

I headed back to the office to say that I was leaving, and as I opened the door and walked in, my eyes were drawn down to the tiny face that was peering at me from behind the manager's legs. Choosing a dog is very much like falling in love. There was something about this particular pup, just as there had been when I had first seen Pepper, that resonated with me. There was something about these two dogs that seemed familiar and I knew that this pup was the one for me.

Even so, never for one moment did I think that this puppy, a Border collie, who was staring intently in my direction, would be looking for a home. It was too beautiful, with striking merle markings, huge ears and the softest, most gentle eyes and expression on its face. The huge ears that seemed too big for the puppy's head were pricked up one minute and then laid flat the next, as it tried to suss me out. I moved forward a few steps, not wanting to get too close and frighten it, but getting just close enough so that when I crouched down, I could see it more clearly. The pup's face was prettily marked, with lots of tiny black splodges breaking up the light grey colour, and a narrow streak of white that went up the centre of its face between its eyes. It had the most adorable and unusual nose I had ever seen. It was pink with two tiny areas of black pigmentation. This would eventually spread until, aged nine years, the whole nose would be completely black. Long, slender white legs and dainty paws caught my eye, and its smooth coat made the merle markings very clear.

I jokingly said, 'I'll take that one if it's available.'

The manager's reply stunned me.

'She's yours if you want her.'

I couldn't believe what I was hearing! Not only was this pup available, but it was also female, which was exactly what I wanted. She embodied every physical characteristic I adored in a dog. I had been fascinated by blue merle markings and the intelligence of Border collies for years. I wasn't expecting to find 'my' blue merle on that day in November, but there she was, and I absolutely wanted her!

The puppy was called Poppy and, it being 11 November, it seemed a fitting name. She was one day off being four months old, and had at that very moment arrived at the dog pound to be rehomed. Was it fate that brought both me and this young pup to the same place at exactly the same time? I believe it was our destiny to be together and forces were at work when Poppy found herself in such a precarious situation that would determine the rest of her life.

This chance meeting was going to be a new start for both of us and I was simultaneously both excited and nervous. Was I ready for a Border collie? Was I going to be able to fulfil her need to be physically and mentally stimulated? This was a huge decision and the weight of the responsibility frightened me a little.

I walked towards her and picked up her lead, which was lying on the floor. I said that I was definitely interested and asked to take her outside. Once we were in the fresh air, I studied this puppy in front of me and I couldn't stop thinking how beautiful she was. I talked to her and tried to get her attention, but she wouldn't listen or turn her gaze towards me. She completely ignored me, despite my best efforts, and it suddenly occurred to me that she might be deaf.

I took her for a little walk down the lane and tried to attract her attention. Despite the myriad weird sounds that I made, from squeaks to whistles, she didn't look at me. I decided there and then that I still wanted her even if she did indeed turn out to be deaf, so I gently picked her up and told her that we'd figure things out together.

We walked back up the lane, this time with me carrying this precious puppy. We stopped by my car and I opened the door to allow Pepper to say hello to her. This was not only my decision; it was Pepper's too. If she didn't like Poppy, then I would have to seriously reconsider. I wasn't too worried about Pepper not liking Poppy, though, as she was always so gentle with young dogs and any animal she met that was smaller than she was – apart from cats, that is, which she detested and would chase, given the slightest opportunity! As long as another dog was friendly, then Pepper was too, but even so, I held my breath while Pepper stretched her nose towards the puppy in my arms. Pepper's ears went up – a good sign – and then she squeaked as she did when something really excited her. Poppy leaned forward to sniff Pepper's nose, but other than that was completely still.

I took Poppy back to the office and said that I almost definitely wanted her. I asked if she could stay at the pound overnight to give me a chance to ask my mum's opinion, though. It was agreed that I could come and collect her at ten the following morning, or phone if I had decided I didn't want her.

I regret having left her at the dog pound that night. I should have taken her home there and then rather than leave her to spend the night in strange surroundings full of scary sounds and unfamiliar smells. I only did it because I wasn't completely confident in my own decision. Mum was my best friend as well as being my mother, and her opinion always mattered and influenced me a great deal. I didn't need her to sanction my decision to get another dog – I had my own flat and was no longer living in her home – but I really wanted her approval.

Mum said she'd come with me to the pound the following day. I was excited but also anxious to see what she would say when she saw Poppy for the first time. Mum took a good look at her. She could see that this puppy was going to be just perfect for me to train to compete in Heelwork to Music competitions and agreed with me about how pretty she was – she approved.

Relieved to have her support, I scooped Poppy up and went into the office. As she had only been there one night, I was told that £10 would suffice in payment. I duly handed over a crumpled ten-pound note, thanked the manager and proudly took Poppy to my car. She seemed glad to be in my arms, leaning into me and wedging her head under my chin.

Mum drove home so I could have Poppy on my lap. Pepper was on the back seat wearing a harness, which attached to the seat belt to keep her safe, and she poked her head over my shoulder to have a look and a sniff. Poppy held very still while Pepper snorted in her ear, although it did startle her, and I had to wipe the side of my face. Pepper again started to make excited squeaking noises and I knew that she liked our new addition.

Poppy was very well behaved for the journey. She stood on my lap looking through the window, and I soon realized that she was not deaf at all! Whenever I spoke to her, she immediately looked up at my face and made eye contact. This was great news. I realized that being at the pound must have affected her behaviour; she had disconnected from everything and completely shut down due to fear. She snuggled into me and from time to time would gently lick my face. I was keen to make her feel loved and safe. In just under four months of her short life, she had had three homes: the first with the comfort of her mother and brothers and sisters, then a new home for a brief eight weeks, followed by a quick and unsettling spell at the dog pound. Now she was coming to her 'for ever home', with me and Pepper. Being dumped in the pound at the age of four months is unimaginable. I was very mindful of the fact that just eight weeks earlier, she had suffered the trauma of being taken from her mother and her siblings, and here she was facing yet another upheaval.

I whispered in her ear that she was safe now and everything was going to be fine. The trust in her soulful brown eyes was obvious and I felt a little tearful when she looked at me. I loved her already, and the way she looked at me told me she was ready to feel the same way.

At one point on the journey home after she had been gazing up at me, I was reminded of our family Labrador, Chandie, who had sadly died four years earlier of liver cancer, not even reaching his tenth birthday. He was fed for years on shop-bought dog food before Mum changed to a more natural brand. I later discovered that the processed food, with its myriad additives, had in all likelihood played a part in his illness.

I was inspired by Mum's organic lifestyle to pay close attention to the food I was feeding Pepper and would now feed this new puppy. I never gave them processed dog food and, after researching alternatives, gave them a totally raw, natural diet of free range meat, bones, offal and pulverized fruit and vegetables, with all of the ingredients organically grown and freshly prepared twice a day. It's not the most convenient way to feed your dog, but I believe without question it is the best.

I wondered what I should call the puppy, who was now exploring in some detail my left ear with her cold, wet nose. Although her name was fitting for the date, I thought she needed a fresh name for a new start and a thought entered my head that she might be Chandie reincarnated. I had loved him very much and remembered all the times we had spent charging around the garden over makeshift agility courses I had cobbled together. In the evenings, he would lie on his back in my arms while I sat on the sofa and stay there for ages until I couldn't take his weight any more.

I asked Mum what she thought about this idea, half expecting her to think that I was being daft.

'Maybe she is Chandie reincarnated, and maybe she isn't, but I don't see why you couldn't call her Chandie.'

So Poppy's name was duly changed to Chandi. I took the 'e' off the end to make the name her own and it seemed to suit her. After just a few times of saying her name, she was looking up at me wearing an expression that said, 'Yes, that's me! What do you want?' Many years later, I learned that *chandi* means 'silver' in Urdu – an appropriate name for my puppy, with her silvery-grey markings.

Even though Chandi had only been in the kennels one

night, she smelt horrible – fear mixed with desperation, combined with overtones of disinfectant. We went to my parents' house to give Chandi a bath and remove the horrible stench. I didn't want to take her straight back to the flat because I wanted to wash her in an outside space so there wouldn't be any of the 'kennel smell' in her new home.

As it was a cold November day, both Mum and Dad had already said they would help, to get it done quickly. Dad was waiting for us to arrive and he came outside to see Chandi as soon as Mum pulled onto the driveway. He liked Chandi straight away and reached out to stroke her. She looked up at him and wagged her tail. Dad loved dogs, and adored Pepper, but wasn't keen on going for walks and all that owning a dog entails. He wasn't much of an outdoors person.

Dad had an old tin bath waiting in the garage. We put Chandi in the warm water and she stood there as good as gold and didn't attempt to move. She was a tiny, long-legged thing, and once she was wet she looked even smaller and decidedly vulnerable. We lathered her up and then rinsed her off as quickly as possible. I towelled her dry and then bundled her up in my coat and a blanket, and put her on the front seat of my car to take her to her new home.

Chandi was good on the journey and listened when I

told her to lie still. She had initially wanted to stand up on the seat and look out of the window, but I thought she would be safer if she lay down. After a bit of encouragement and me gently holding her down with one hand, she understood and stopped trying to stand up. She gave a little sigh and, placing her pink nose between her front paws, drifted off to sleep.

When we got back to our flat, Pepper bounced out of the car in her usual energetic and flamboyant style, with her long, wavy fur blowing in the wind. I gently lifted Chandi out of the car and carried her up the steep stairs, while Pepper galloped ahead. I opened the front door and put Chandi down so Pepper could get a really good look at her. I knew Pepper was excited about Chandi being in our home by the way she was looking at me and repeatedly squeaking.

Suddenly, Chandi did a little play bow to Pepper and as quick as a flash turned tail and ran across the living room floor with Pepper in hot pursuit. They chased each other around the living room until they were both so hot and exhausted that they flopped down on the floor side by side; then Chandi promptly fell asleep.

From the moment Chandi walked into her new home, it was as though she had always been with us. She copied Pepper's good behaviour, and I loved watching the fun they had playing together. There was never a cross word between them, and with two dog beds next to my bed, our home looked rather cosy.

Every morning we would walk to the end of the road where we lived, down through the wood and into the valley. As soon as I let Pepper off her lead, she would rush off to explore, but Chandi would stay close to me. I kept her on her lead for our first walk, but she didn't want to leave my side anyway. The second day, I decided that since she was responding so well to her name and eagerly coming to me when I called her, I would see how she reacted off the lead. Once Chandi realized that she had some freedom, she started scampering around, but never moving more than a few feet away from me. I crouched down and, with my arms open wide, called her to me. The instant she heard her name, she flung herself round and galloped over, skidding to a halt in front of me. I closed my arms around her and gently gave her a hug, telling her how good she was. From day one Chandi has never let me out of her sight, and she has never left mine.

Chandi was more reserved and cautious than Pepper, who was a real tomboy. Pepper was always ready for a challenge and would fling herself wholeheartedly into any task with huge enthusiasm. Chandi, in contrast, liked to consider things carefully before attempting anything and sometimes needed encouragement.

The first time Chandi encountered water, she was frightened. Having been used to Pepper charging through any depth of water, I was not expecting Chandi to refuse to cross a shallow stream. Pepper ran straight through, gleefully splashing as much water as she possibly could, while I hopped from stepping stone to stepping stone and onto the path on the far side. I suddenly realized Chandi wasn't by me any longer and turned to see where she was. Looking over my shoulder, I spotted her sat with her ears down, looking thoroughly miserable on the other side. I called her to come to me and she got up, dipped a toe in the water, then backed away again. I had started to make my way back to her when Pepper thundered past me. She stood next to Chandi and nudged her forward with her shoulder. Step by step, Chandi let Pepper guide and encourage her across. As soon as Chandi's paws were on dry land again, Pepper raced off to search for rabbits in the bracken without a backward glance, and from that day onwards Chandi never hesitated to cross a stream.

The Christmas tree didn't last long that year. My flat was small, but I adored it – it had everything we needed. However, it was just too small for both the tree and the newly designated racetrack round the sofa next to it, so I had the tree packed away by the middle of December as they kept knocking it over. By the time I'd decorated it six times, it was starting to get a bit tedious.

Mum and Dad invited us round to Orchard House for Christmas Day and I bundled all the presents I'd bought for Pepper, Chandi, Mum and Dad into the car, along with their two dog beds. Watching both dogs tear into their presents and then clearing up all the tiny pieces of wrapping paper they had enjoyed playing tug of war with took a while, but the atmosphere was happy. After lunch, Mum and I went for a walk across the fields with Pepper and Chandi, while Dad stayed at home by the fire. It wasn't long before we joined him, both dogs snoozing in their beds in the living room.

Once the festivities were over for the day, I took my little family back home. I didn't mind not having a tree, as it was so entertaining watching my two gorgeous dogs having fun that nothing else mattered. It was like being in the middle of a Tom and Jerry cartoon. I knew that I'd made the right decision in bringing Chandi to live with us.

In the days that followed, Chandi continued to settle in really well. With Pepper's help, she made herself right at home and quickly became comfortable enough to sleep anywhere in the flat.

Late one evening, I noticed her sitting upright on the

living room floor with her eyes shut. I had no idea she was asleep until I saw her head dropping forward! When her chin hit her chest, she woke and looked round, wide-eyed and startled. A second later, her eyes were tight shut again and her head was starting to loll to one side. She looked so sweet falling asleep while trying to sit up. I went over and scooped her up in my arms, then placed her gently in her bed. Giving a small contented sigh, she curled her legs under her and was soon fast asleep.

The only thing Chandi really asked of me as a puppy, and indeed the only thing she has ever asked of me, was quite simple: I was to please not leave her on her own. Trips to the bathroom have never been the same since Chandi came into my life; she likes to have access to me at all times, and in the early days a shut door meant that she would throw back her head and howl. For something so small and dainty, the tremendous noise that came from deep within her was extremely primitive and, living in a flat with neighbours in such close proximity, completely unacceptable. The problem was easily solved at home, as long as I remembered to leave the door ajar when I went into another room. Unfortunately I wasn't always at home and had to leave both dogs in order to teach music at my parents' house, so to start with, I was nervous about Chandi's howling upsetting the neighbours. I needn't have worried, though, as strangely she never made a sound while I was away. She felt secure with Pepper and I would come home to find them both fast asleep. They wouldn't just sleep while I was away: the whole floor would be strewn with their many toys and it certainly looked as though they'd been having fun.

Soon after I brought Chandi into our lives, I was absolutely delighted to receive the invite from the Kennel Club for Pepper and me to perform our Heelwork to Music routine at Discover Dogs at Earls Court, thanks to being placed third in our very first Heelwork to Music competition seven months earlier. This was quite an honour.

The day of the show came and I drove Pepper and Chandi down to London. I was thrilled and very proud to be walking into the show with my two beautiful dogs. This was the first time Pepper and I had been to such a huge show, and it was Chandi's first time at a show of any description. Pepper was excited too and was prancing sideways towards the entrance, like a mini racehorse. Chandi was walking sensibly, staying close to me, but looking around with interest. Nothing was fazing either dog, though, I was pleased to see.

We queued up with all the other dogs and handlers, waiting to show our entry tickets. Once we were inside, I found where we were benched. The 'benching' is a very long, wide plank of wood raised off the ground and divided into sections so each dog can have its own individual compartment. I proceeded to make the dogs a comfortable bed with a heavy blanket over the top of the benching, which muffles some of the noise and stops the harsh glare of the lights. I know this for a fact because I've tried it out myself!

When it was Pepper's turn to perform in the main ring, I told Chandi to be good and started to walk away. By the time I'd walked just three paces, the howling started and every eye turned to look at Chandi and me, much to my horror. I felt embarrassed, to say the least, and despite my best attempts at trying to shush her, every time I stepped away with Pepper, she would start up again. As I was there on my own, I wasn't quite sure what to do, and we were due in the ring to perform.

Fortunately a kind man came to my rescue and said that he would sit with Chandi while Pepper and I performed, as he could keep an eye on his own dogs at the same time. At times, Chandi's howling was still audible above the music when Pepper and I were in the ring, but Pepper seemed oblivious and enjoyed performing our routine, throwing her head back and exaggerating many of the movements. It was a very proud moment for both of us, but I was anxious to get back to Chandi, as I hated knowing that she was distressed.

I wasn't surprised that Chandi hated it when Pepper and I left her; it was surely due to all the upheaval Chandi had experienced in just a few short months of life. She was obviously afraid of being abandoned again. As the years went by and Chandi realized I always came back, she stopped howling for me, but at that moment I wished I could make her understand that she needn't worry and that I was never going to abandon her.

After giving Chandi some time to settle into her new life with me and Pepper and adjust to her new routine, I started to work with her a little every day, teaching her basic obedience and then the tricks that I had first taught Pepper. She was incredibly attentive and extremely keen to learn. She perfected all the tricks and moves I taught her and mastered them very quickly. I was becoming better at conveying exactly what I needed Chandi to do, and our ability to communicate was set to lead us both down a fascinating road of discovery.

Pepper's beautiful heelwork had taken a long time to perfect, but Chandi took up the watchful position by my side naturally. At just a few months old, she was getting herself into the heel position on my left and turning her head to the right so she could look up at me. More than just getting herself into position, she was lifting each of her front paws very high as we moved and producing the most stylish trot, flinging her paws out with each step. Of course, at first she couldn't hold the exact position next to my left leg without surging forward in excitement, but over the coming weeks I taught her to hold the position close to me for longer, keeping her shoulders level at all times. I praised her to the skies when she was in the correct position, naming it 'close'.

Each day we practised we were able to extend the amount of time she would maintain the perfect position. I was delighted with how quickly Chandi's stylish heelwork was developing, and as well as just working with her close to my left leg, we very soon started working on holding the correct position while working close to my right leg as well.

Heelwork to Music is an exciting dog sport not only for the spectators but also for the participants. I always remind myself when starting to work on a new routine that the only thing that limits you is lack of imagination. If you can envisage your dog doing something fantastic and then you can figure out how to teach your dog what you are imagining, you are on to something fabulous.

One tempis were the first complex thing I wanted to teach Chandi and I set about showing her what I wanted when she was about five months old. We practised a lot and very soon she was getting nicely into the skipping rhythm. I couldn't believe that I'd managed to teach Chandi as well as Pepper to do this, and it became one of the signature moves in our routines.

The feeling of sheer joy I experience each and every time Chandi and I skip side by side has never diminished over the years. It is the most amazing feeling, and I can see by the expression on her face that Chandi certainly feels how special this is as well. It felt the same with Pepper too.

With Chandi's heelwork coming along beautifully and the one tempis perfected, it was time to try and put together a routine with her for the annual Heelwork to Music competition held by Rugby Dog Training Club. The competition was in April, and it was already January. I had continued to work with Pepper and her new routine, to 'Singing in the Rain', was also coming along nicely. Chandi was only going to be nine months old in April, and we'd have been together for just five months, so I did wonder if I was a little crazy contemplating entering her, but it would be good experience for her if nothing else.

The more I worked with Chandi, the closer we became and we both looked forward to our training sessions. I am very vocal when working with my dogs and the energy that emanates from me passes on to them and motivates them to give their all. We are always exhausted after we've worked together, but it is a satisfying feeling.

I was still working on my training methods, of course, and adapting them to Pepper's and Chandi's quite different characters. Pepper needed to be motivated and inspired to engage with me, but when she did and I had managed to excite her and infuse her with energy, she was wonderfully flamboyant with her movements. She would toss her head, making her long fur rise and fall, and a huge grin would spread across her face. Chandi, on the other hand, was keener to work, but she was very sensitive, and if she sensed that I wasn't happy with something, she would become clingy and upset.

As I explained earlier, I had realized years back that keeping everything positive was the only way to motivate Pepper to really want to work with me, and the same was now true for Chandi. To be trying so hard and then have a mistake met with disappointment is no way to build trust and enthusiasm. Working in a strange environment at a competition is stressful and a real test of the mutual trust you have built up. To attempt a competition with Chandi after only knowing each other for five months was going to be the ultimate test for us both.

At the beginning of March 1999, a month before the Rugby Dog Training Club competition, Pepper was due to perform a routine in the special events ring at Crufts.

It was my dream to perform at Crufts, a dream shared by many dog trainers all over the world. Seeing an opportunity to get Pepper on television, I rang the BBC and asked to speak to a researcher working on their coverage of Crufts. I told the researcher about Pepper's start in life and how she'd been rescued from a local pound – now she was to perform at Crufts. They decided to feature a story about her, and on 15 February 1999, a camera crew drove up to Shropshire to film us for the programme.

They arrived at our flat and we all went up onto the moorland, the Long Mynd, together as it would provide a beautiful backdrop for the interview. It was, however, a punishingly cold day and I knew that we would be hanging around outside for hours, so I piled as many layers on as I could.

Pepper behaved impeccably during most of the interview, but as the filming took quite a while, she did get bored at one point and decided that she would rather do something more interesting. She got up from where she had been sitting next to me, yawned directly into the camera and walked away, much to everyone's amusement.

The second part of the interview was to take place at Crufts itself. I was delighted to be doing some more television, and particularly thrilled that I was to do it with the love of my life, Pepper.

Arriving at the NEC (National Exhibition Centre) in

Birmingham for Crufts, I had never seen so many dogs, and as we made the long walk from the car park, both Pepper and Chandi behaved perfectly. The atmosphere in the hall was electric, and the noise of dogs barking, people talking and music playing was quite deafening. Pepper and Chandi just took everything in their stride, though.

We found the benching area allocated to us and I settled both dogs and made them comfortable, again with a blanket over the top of the bench to muffle the noise and shut out some of the strong lighting.

I suddenly felt a tap on my shoulder and a voice said, 'Hello, Tina! When you're ready, can we do some more filming with you and Pepper getting ready to go into the ring, please?'

I turned round to see the BBC producer we had worked with a few weeks before standing there with the rest of the crew. I answered, 'Yes, of course. Give me two seconds and we'll be with you,' but my stomach lurched. This was added pressure, but would make our first time at Crufts even more memorable.

Pepper and I prepared ourselves and, recalling Chandi's distress and subsequent howling when we left her on the bench at our previous performance, I asked the kind lady next to us if she would sit with her and stroke her, which she was more than happy to do.

It was a very proud moment for me walking into the arena with Pepper by my side and performing our routine to 'Singing in the Rain'. I couldn't help thinking about how far we had come and how special it was to see Pepper, this gorgeous dog, oozing with confidence, strutting by my side. She was so very different from the miserable wreck I'd brought home from the dog pound.

As well as helping Pepper overcome her truly awful start to life, working together had given me a fresh focus. It gave me a chance to examine myself in detail and decide exactly who I wanted to be. I've come to understand that whatever situation we are in, there is always something to learn. It is our choice, though, as to whether or not we decide to make a change, learn and grow. I carefully watched how my behaviour impacted on Pepper and I wanted to be the best I could be for her sake. I expected a lot from her and it was only fair that I gave as much as I could in return. I was learning patience and respect, and I appreciated just how hard Pepper was working, even when things didn't go quite right. I truly valued everything she had brought to my life since we met, and I absolutely adored her.

Our first time at Crufts was a momentous experience and I was overwhelmed by all the emotions that suddenly welled up in me as we left the ring after performing. I crouched down to hug Pepper and she saw immediately that I was crying and licked the tears from my face. They were tears of pure joy that we shared that day.

A month after Crufts, in April 1999, the day of the annual Heelwork to Music show dawned. We had worked so hard on our routines. Chandi and Pepper were performing in different classes – Chandi was in intermediate and Pepper in advanced. Chandi was to go first.

Waiting with Chandi for our turn in the ring, I felt anxious. I had to change my emotions, though, as Chandi was looking up at me with her ears clamped down against her head. She was sensing my mood and it was worrying her. Both Pepper and Chandi were so sensitive to how I was feeling that if I was ever upset over something, they would come running over and place themselves on either side of me, pushing their little faces into me to comfort me. On the other hand, when I was really happy, they would act like lunatics, running around and jumping on me and then chasing each other in circles, until finally I couldn't just stand and watch them any longer and would have to join in with the game.

Right now, though, I needed to get energized and try to lift us both and motivate Chandi to fly through her routine. It was up to me to turn this around. I needed Chandi's first experience of a competition to be a good one, otherwise it could make her anxious at future events.

I managed to rally myself and be positive as Chandi and I were warming up outside the ring and I saw her start to relax. Her ears were no longer flat against her head but upright, and she focused her attention fully on me as we did some heelwork. I praised her until her tail was wagging furiously and she knew she was doing well.

We got through our routine pretty faultlessly except for one major omission. I realized as we were leaving the ring that I had forgotten to put in the one tempis, the skipping move we had worked so hard to perfect before the competition. How could I have been so stupid?

I was incredibly chuffed when we were awarded third place, though I couldn't help but wonder if we could have achieved more. It wasn't bad going after such a short time together and I knew we had more to offer – there were those damn one tempis for a start!

Pepper's routine also went well, but again I knew we could do better. I decided there and then to come back better and stronger with both dogs the next year.

The following year, 2000, was a good one and all our hard work and dedication seemed to be paying off. I continued to work with Pepper and Chandi on new moves for our routines and I felt we were improving all the time. Chandi was particularly striking in her attitude to training, and we both adored the complete focus and attention we had for each other while working.

When I wasn't teaching, I spent all my time in the company of my dogs, and Mum would come over several times a week to walk out on the Long Mynd with us. I was always keen to show her the latest moves I'd taught both the dogs, and she would applaud our efforts, amazed at the things we were doing. Mum featured largely in my life and we would speak on the phone at least once a day, if not four or five times.

At the 2000 Rugby Dog Training Club show, Chandi was again entered in the intermediate class. Our routine, set to a piece of jive music, was awarded first place, and moved us out of intermediate into advanced. I was delighted to have won the class, but I was also disappointed. Chandi had performed brilliantly, but what I had tried to create with the routine hadn't come across as I had anticipated.

I realized I was frustrated. I wasn't frustrated with Chandi, though – she had been fantastic – I was frustrated with myself. I was in charge of creating the routines; Chandi could only ever do what I asked of her, or so I thought. Looking back, I wonder if somewhere inside me I knew the kind of routines we were going to produce in the future, that were going to push the boundaries of Heelwork to Music, with its close precision work, and the newly emerging category of Freestyle, which gave more opportunity to showcase tricks and moves. I just needed to find a way to tap into the possibilities and propel us both to new heights.

I knew that whatever I came up with, Chandi would match me step for step, and as it turned out, she was to become my inspiration when she inadvertently took charge of our training session one day and created her own stunning move. I had accidentally given her the wrong command while she was on her hind legs and instead of doing what I intended, she did something she had never done before. She reversed up to me, only coming to a halt once her back was touching mine. I was stunned, and suddenly an image flashed into my mind of how this would look to someone watching and I asked Chandi to turn. This was something else she had never done up on her hind legs, but with me steadying her a little, we both began to turn, slowly at first and then faster as Chandi realized she could do what I was now asking.

This was what was to become our famous back-to-back move. It was Chandi showing me something I would never have dreamed possible that opened my mind to then go on to invent more new moves that had never before been seen in competition. Our next routine was to be one of the defining moments of our lives and was to turn Chandi and me into two of the brightest stars in Heelwork to Music. Other competitors around the world would try to emulate the moves we invented with varying degrees of success and put them into their own routines.

Three

A Frightening Diagnosis

Late September 2000 was very exciting for us. For the first time, there were two large Heelwork to Music competitions that I wanted to go to that year and one was in Jersey. Lately, shows had been springing up across the country, but I didn't want to compete at all of them. I liked having just one prestigious show to aim for each year – the big one organized by the Rugby Dog Training Club – and immediately after the competition I would begin working on new moves and ideas for the following year's routine. This new competition in Jersey, though, seemed like an opportunity not to be missed.

I had become friends with Donelda Guy, the organizer of the show, who was also a Heelwork to Music competitor, and she had kindly arranged for me and the dogs to stay with her friend Jean. Jean generously offered to have us for a couple of extra days and I jumped at the chance to extend what was really a busman's holiday into a real holiday. This meant that Pepper, Chandi and I would be able to relax and go exploring before and after the competition. I booked the ferry crossing to Jersey, which, despite being expensive, seemed like a great adventure for me, Pepper and Chandi to share. This would be the longest trip we had ever been on together.

Pepper and Chandi were excited when they saw me pack a suitcase and start to load the car with their beds, toys and food, as well as my suitcase and the costumes needed for our routines. They knew something was up and watched in anticipation. Both dogs loved travelling in the car and were very good passengers. Once they were bored with watching the world go by through the window, they would contentedly fall asleep, both lying on the back seat of the car wearing their harnesses.

By the time we had got to Poole and joined the queue of cars waiting to board the ferry, my excitement had dwindled somewhat. The weather was appalling and the sea looked really rough. This was Pepper's and Chandi's first time on a ferry and I wondered if they would be OK. They would have to stay in the car below deck throughout the journey, with the windows slightly open, while I went above, but I was allowed to check on them provided I was taken down by an escort. However, sitting in that queue as the rain pelted against the car, I was fast losing my nerve and I very nearly turned the car round and drove the four and a half hours back home. I couldn't chicken out, though, and decided just to get on the ferry, thinking to myself: How bad could it actually be?

We had atrocious weather conditions for most of the journey and I felt terribly seasick. Up on deck, I found it almost impossible to keep my balance as the ferry was tossed in every direction. I was worried about leaving Pepper and Chandi alone during such a stomach-churning journey, but I think they slept most of the way and they seemed perfectly happy when I checked on them.

By the time we reached Jersey, the sea was much calmer and the weather was gloriously sunny. Jersey looked absolutely beautiful. We disembarked from the ferry and headed for Jean's house.

Having only spoken to Jean on the phone, I was a little worried, but as soon as we arrived, I felt as though I had known her for years. She was so welcoming and even cleared a shelf in her fridge so I could keep the dogs' fresh food cool. I loved hearing her speak in her authentic Jersey accent. Her house was very comfortable and Pepper and Chandi seemed extremely relaxed there. Jean was happy for us to come and go as we pleased, which suited us perfectly.

We had a day and a half free before the competition, so we went to explore the island. Knowing how much

Pepper loved the beach, I asked Jean if she could recommend one and she suggested St Ouen's, on the west of the island. Packing some lunch for us all, and with the windows wound right down in the car, we headed straight there. Both dogs had a wonderful time running along the shore and chasing the seagulls before racing back to tell me all about the fun they were having.

They took it in turns to come and practise parts of their competition routines, each lying down patiently to watch while the other worked with me. With the wind in our hair and the sun on our backs, life was absolutely perfect right then, and we were all relaxed and happy.

The first time Mum and I had taken Pepper to the beach was about a year after I had rescued her. We took her to our favourite beach on the West Wales coast, situated between Barmouth and Harlech, a very beautiful stretch of sand backed by huge dunes. Dogs are allowed on one section of it during the summer months. I don't think Pepper had seen the sea or the sand before, because she started to run around excitedly the moment we got there. It was a windy June day but beautifully warm, and it wasn't long before Pepper decided that the beach belonged to her and that no seagull was allowed to land on it. She proceeded to make it her mission to run at every one that landed and chase it away. Getting braver, she was even running into the sea to stop them landing there and at times was no bigger than a speck on the horizon. She was so funny to watch, and Mum and I were in fits of laughter, and genuinely in awe of her energy and determination.

One section of this particular beach is designated a nudist area and in order to have a long walk with Pepper, we had to navigate our way through many, many naked people. I always find it quite surprising the number of people who are comfortable getting their kit off in public! However, my beautiful, energetic but slightly wayward dog thought naked people were just the best thing ever. She was, by now, bored with the pesky seagulls and looking for a new activity. She proceeded to make her own fun by running up to anyone she didn't like the look of and barking at them. She would then chase them up the beach until she lost interest or someone else took her fancy.

I know that I should have gone to fetch Pepper back, but I was both too weak from laughing so much and slightly embarrassed about having to approach anyone without their clothes on. Despite my conscience telling me to go and fetch Pepper, I just couldn't do it, so Mum and I decided that the best thing to do was turn round and head back down the beach.

A little while later, we heard the screams suddenly stop and then Pepper was right beside me, grinning up at us with sand all over her face. She didn't stay by my side long; shortly after, she rushed to the sea and started to drink. I ran over to her to stop her drinking the salty water and pulled her away, but she kept returning again and again. Poor Pepper was so thirsty after all her fun and games that she kept heading for the sea and managed to drink a little each time before I could stop her.

When we got back to the car, it was getting late and we hadn't had any lunch. I suggested Pepper might like to lie down for a bit and filled her bowl with water. One bowl wasn't enough, and after refilling it, and watching Pepper almost drain that one too, I didn't feed her straight away but let her rest for a while.

Mum was setting up our picnic when Pepper leapt to her feet and projectile-vomited a vast amount of water mixed with sand. I had told her that drinking sea water was not a good idea, but I guess she had to learn the hard way.

When we arrived home, I let Pepper into the house while Mum and I unloaded the car. As I was walking up the hall to the kitchen with the picnic basket, I could hear Pepper drinking, but she wasn't anywhere near her water bowl. Walking back up the hall, I soon found her. Pepper was standing with her head in the toilet and was drinking furiously. I guess for Pepper it was a perfect end to what had been an absolutely tremendous day!

This trip to the beach in Jersey, though, passed without incident and it was lovely running through our routines on the sand. For the competition the next day, I was doing a routine to Bert Kaempfert's 'Swinging Safari' with Chandi, and Pepper's was to 'Cotton-Eyed Joe'. We performed brilliantly that day, with Chandi winning her class and Pepper coming second.

We enjoyed the next two days exploring more of Jersey's wonderful beaches, and when it came time to leave, I was very sad. We had enjoyed our holiday immensely, and after presenting Jean with a huge box of chocolates to thank her for her hospitality and giving her a hug, the dogs and I headed back to the ferry port for the long journey home.

Back in Shropshire, I had a phone call from our local BBC news programme, who had heard about the 'dancing-dog show' and Chandi's performance. They wanted to feature both Pepper and Chandi on the programme and as a result Chandi was also invited to do a short performance on our region's *Children in Need*. This involved taking a trip to BBC Pebble Mill Studios in Birmingham to meet the producer and show him what we could do before the live programme the following week. On the grass outside Pebble Mill, Chandi showed off her best moves in an edited version of our 'Swinging Safari' routine, and the producer loved it.

Mum came with us for the proper performance and I was glad of the moral support; this was the first time we had ever done live television and I was trying not to think about it. Every time I did I started to feel sick with nerves. Chandi had never even been inside a television studio before and I was worried about how she would react.

To my relief, Chandi did really well, especially for her first time in a studio. Mum stood at the back and watched the whole thing. We got through the performance, but I knew that my nerves had dampened down Chandi's energy – she didn't sparkle like I knew she could. Nonetheless it was a good first experience for both of us and we enjoyed ourselves. I was glad to get back to Pepper, who had been patiently waiting in the dressing room while we had been in the studio. It felt like we had been away for hours, but Mum told me it was only fifteen minutes!

Just a couple of months after our expedition to Jersey, Chandi and Pepper were due to appear at the Kennel Club's Discover Dogs in Earls Court once more. Being invited to perform at the show was a special honour and only four or five of the top dogs and handlers received an invite in those early years. To my surprise, Dad said he wanted to come with us and help out with the driving; this was the first time he had come to see us perform. He hadn't been feeling very well for a couple of months with a painful throat that, despite visiting the doctor, didn't seem to be getting better. Dad didn't make a big deal about his throat, but Mum had told me on the phone the night before that it was really bothering him. She had sounded worried and that worried me too. Dad had dismissed it when I asked him about it. I think he didn't want to concern me.

I was glad of the company on the journey to London, and having Dad in the audience for support was lovely. Both Pepper and Chandi gave great performances in the noisy arena and we enjoyed the day. Chandi and Pepper were each awarded a crystal trophy as a souvenir of the event. We were very tired when we got home, especially Dad, who had driven us all the way home through torrential rain. Little did we know then that his fatigue was due to more than just the long, tiring drive.

Just before Christmas that year, Dad returned to the doctor about his painful throat and he arranged for Dad to see a specialist at the hospital. The appointment was for the middle of January and Dad was told not to worry as it probably wasn't anything serious, but it was on our minds over Christmas. When Dad finally saw the consultant, he booked him in to return for a biopsy a week later.

The results of the biopsy revealed that Dad had throat

cancer, and major surgery was needed to remove the tumour. It was possible that he would need a course of radiotherapy as well. Dad was booked in for his operation on 14 February 2001, and the night before he told me he loved me. I don't remember him ever saying that to me before and in that moment I felt closer to my dad than I had in the whole of my life.

The operation Dad was to undergo was very invasive and involved cutting through his lower lip and jaw bone so the surgeon could reach the tumour at the back of his throat. After the operation, Dad would be transferred straight to intensive care and would spend at least a night there before being moved to the ward.

Mum and I went with Dad to the hospital the next morning and sat with him until it was time for the operation. While we were there, the surgeon came to speak to Dad, and I will never forget him saying, 'Don't worry, Mr Humphrey, we'll get it all.'

I remember thinking: How can you be so sure?

Mum and I wished Dad luck, and as we walked up the ward, I turned to wave to him. He looked frail, and despite his outwardly brave appearance, he must have been so frightened. I know I was.

The operation lasted about five hours and finally the hospital called to say that Dad was recovering in the intensive care unit. Although he had said beforehand that he didn't want me to see him hooked up to all the machines and with his face unrecognizable from the operation, I wanted to go and so Mum and I went together.

Dad was very sleepy but did wake up a little bit and tried to talk. He was obviously in a lot of discomfort, but he had a syringe driver with morphine in his arm and he could use the 'boost' button to give him slightly more relief if he needed it. It was absolutely awful seeing him like that and I was glad when he was moved to the ward. After a few days, he started to feel a little better as the intense pain eased and he began to heal.

When Dad was discharged from the hospital, he was feeling much better and he was enjoying being at home. Things seemed fine, and most importantly the soreness in his throat was gone.

Everything, however, was far from fine and at his next appointment with the consultant Dad was told that the margins around the tumour they had removed were very small and there was a chance that they hadn't got it all out. He would have to undergo weeks of radiotherapy treatment to try to kill the remaining cancer cells.

By now it was April 2001 and it was once more time for the huge Heelwork to Music show held by Rugby Dog Training Club near Coventry. Training had been really difficult that year, as we were in the middle of the horrible foot-and-mouth outbreak and had no access to any of our usual open spaces to train. I was finding my dad's illness and the gut-wrenching pictures of all the slaughtered animals in the media incredibly difficult to cope with. For me, the whole world seemed to have turned on its head. It was only when I was busy training and working with Pepper and Chandi that I was able to forget about how worried I was over Dad's illness.

Because of the foot-and-mouth epidemic, the only place I could think of to use to train with the dogs was the school playing field a short distance from my house, so we started getting up at 5.30 a.m. every day in order to be off the field before anyone saw us and told us to stop.

I had seen Donelda Guy's dog perform several moves on her hind legs at the previous year's Heelwork to Music competition. The one that caught my eye was where the dog went behind Donelda and rested her front paws on her back. They then both walked forward in that position. I could see that there was much more that was potentially possible with Chandi working on her hind legs, so we worked hard on extending that simple move I had seen Donelda introduce. As well as Chandi following behind me with her paws resting on my back as though we were doing the conga, I taught Chandi to then do a 180-degree turn on her hind legs so she was facing in the opposite direction. As she turned, I turned too, so now Chandi was leading the conga. One of the hardest things to teach a dog to do is to move away from you. To ask Chandi not only to move away from me but move away with her back to me, and more importantly not to try and turn to look at me as she moved, only increased the difficulty.

Once we had mastered this sequence of moves by practising each part individually before putting them all together, I knew that we had something special that was going to produce a good reaction from the audience. I could imagine their surprise as Chandi turned to lead the dance. I adored our new back-to-back move as well, and I was excited about the competition. I hoped that the amount of dedicated effort we had put into it was going to be worth it. The first time anyone would see the routine and our new moves would be the day of the competition.

Despite being very poorly, Dad said he wanted to come to the show and I was very grateful for the incredible effort it must have taken him to come and support me. He and Mum got up early that Saturday so they would be ready when I arrived at their house. Mum drove their car and followed as I led the way. It only took an hour and a half to reach the show, but it must have been exhausting for Dad. I hoped that he would have a good day and get some pleasure from seeing us perform.

We arrived before 9 a.m. in order for Mum and Dad to get good seats in the second row, but the class I was in wasn't until around four o'clock in the afternoon. It was going to be a long day for all of us, especially Dad. The day seemed to go by very slowly for me, as I couldn't wait to get in the ring and I suddenly felt nervous about the level of difficulty of our new routine. I thought about all the training we had done and the countless times we had been through the whole routine and Chandi had not put a paw wrong. I reminded myself that as long as *I* was confident, then Chandi would be too.

Finally the moment arrived for us to walk into the ring, and with Chandi ready to go and looking up at me intently, I walked forward as she pranced by my side. Waiting for the music to start, I felt nervous, but as soon as we had taken our first steps together, I had no time to think about anything other than the complexity of the movements and giving Chandi all the correct cues.

Chandi was performing absolutely perfectly, and our back-to-back move, along with the other hind-leg moves we'd invented, seemed to go down very well with the audience, who clapped in all the right places throughout the routine. Their spontaneous applause boosted my confidence and Chandi and I were buzzing with excitement by the time we reached the end.

We were awarded second place that year, which was fantastic, as my little ten-pound rescue dog was placed higher than Mary Ray, who was a leading competitor and had the honour of performing a routine before 'Best in Show' was announced at Crufts each year. As far as I was concerned, things were heading in a direction that felt right and very exciting. There was no sense of frustration this year, just a feeling of contentment and satisfaction that all our inventiveness – both mine and Chandi's – and our effort had truly been worthwhile. I was so glad Mum and Dad had both been there to see it.

Dad's radiotherapy treatments continued, and after just a week or so, the appalling side effects began to take their toll. The radiation destroyed Dad's salivary glands, which made eating almost impossible, talking difficult and his mouth constantly dry and uncomfortable. Even if the treatment had killed the cancer cells left in his throat, this was irreparable damage and would last for the rest of his life.

I watched Dad lose the will to live from this point onwards. Despite the treatment, he became ill again. Unable to eat, he underwent minor surgery to insert a tube directly into his stomach so liquid food could bypass his throat.

During this time, Pepper would always be on hand to

sit on my lap and let me hug her whenever I was feeling sad. Chandi didn't like to be hugged like Pepper did, but she would come and sit beside us and lean in close so she could give me little licks on the side of my face with her catlike tongue. The dogs had an amazing way of sensing when I needed some extra love and I remember cuddling up with both of them, hoping Dad would miraculously get better.

After further tests, though, we received the worst news: the cancer had spread to his liver and he was now terminally ill. With Dad becoming progressively worse, Mum wasn't strong enough to look after him at home, and just six months after his surgery to remove the tumour, Dad was moved to a room in the local hospice. Mum and I would take it in turns to visit him, but he was too poorly to talk and barely knew we were there. He had been unconscious almost continuously since he arrived.

It was during this time, just as I was about to leave home to teach a class, when I, and the rest of the world, watched an unbelievable event unfold on the television: the first plane had been flown into the Twin Towers in the terrorist attacks of 9/11. That year had been one of the worst of my life and the world indeed was a very troubled place.

Just two days later, on 13 September 2001, Dad died,

aged sixty-five. I was twenty-nine. Mum and I were with him when he died and I kissed his forehead as he took his last breath. We had never really got to know each other, and now it was too late.

Four

Losing My Best Friend

Dad's death, and indeed his illness, had come as a shock. Seeing how quickly the disease took his life frightened me; Mum had been living with her cancer for over eight years by that time and had enjoyed decent health since her diagnosis. However, the tumour had been steadily increasing in size and I was suddenly more terrified for her. She wasn't currently showing any life-threatening symptoms, and was managing fine, but I was worried about her living on her own after Dad died.

We talked about her options, one of which was to sell up and move to a smaller, more manageable house. I didn't want her to do that – she loved her garden. Mum would spend hour upon hour planting seeds, tending to the large vegetable garden and dead-heading the flowers in her extremely pretty herbaceous borders. Dad used to come out to dig the soil and help prepare the ground for planting, but apart from that the garden was exclusively

Mum's territory, and she was at her happiest when she was in it. I didn't want her to lose it.

Instead I suggested that I sell my flat and move back in with her. Mum was very reluctant at first. She knew what it meant for me and the dogs to have our own space, and we'd just watched Dad suffer so painfully. We both understood that she would eventually become ill and it wasn't going to be easy. I didn't want to give up my flat, but this was more important and I convinced her. At some point, Mum would need me more than ever and I wanted to be there for her. I can't imagine how she must have felt watching Dad die of the same disease – it had been a horrific experience for all of us.

It wasn't an ideal arrangement. I wasn't overjoyed to give up my home, but then it wasn't really an ordinary situation. Of course, I would have loved Mum to be healthy, but she wasn't and the whole point of my coming back to Shropshire after university was to be there for her if and when she needed me. I hadn't just said that without intending to follow through on it; I loved my mum dearly and I really was going to be there for her, whatever that entailed.

Together we came up with the idea of making Pepper, Chandi and me our own space out of two of the upstairs bedrooms in Orchard House. I paid for a small kitchen to be put in and made the place our own. I was so glad that Mum had agreed, as it was a weight off my mind to be closer to her. I finally managed to sell my flat, but looking back, if I'd known what the next two years had in store, I would have kept hold of it.

With our new home ready, Pepper, Chandi and I moved back in on 16 December 2001 and life regained what was to be a short-lived sense of normality. Pepper and Chandi were used to the house, having been there so often, so it wasn't a huge upheaval for them. I was still teaching the piano and violin, but now only had to nip downstairs to work instead of making a twenty-mile round trip. It was nice to have the dogs close by while I worked, and I could often hear them playing together and flinging all their toys around upstairs in our living room while I gave a lesson. Mum no longer worried about the stair carpet getting dirty with the dogs going up and down, but I was still careful always to dry their paws before they were allowed anywhere near the carpet. Pepper and Chandi would patiently wait while I towelled their paws before bounding happily up the stairs.

Just a couple of weeks after we'd moved in, Mum started to complain about a pain in her hip. The pain was intermittent to begin with and I did what I could to help her around the house and in the garden. I also used the Bowen Technique to reduce her pain – a few years earlier, I had done the first part of a course and had regularly used the technique on Mum to help relieve headaches and other minor ailments. I continued to use this treatment on her and it helped with the pain for short periods of time. It was lovely to be able to do something practical for her and I was only too glad to help in this small way. Pepper and Chandi would usually be playing upstairs while I treated Mum, and we would giggle at the bumps on the ceiling and the muffled growls as they threw their toys around.

I didn't think too much about the pain in her hip. Perhaps naively, I thought it would just get better. But it didn't. By the time April came and it was once more time for the best and biggest Heelwork to Music and Freestyle show in the country, held by Rugby Dog Training Club, Mum was decidedly uncomfortable. She was finding walking very painful and the only time she could get any relief, other than when I used the Bowen Technique on her, was if she had her lower back pressed hard up against the back of a chair.

I drove us to the show, but Mum was finding it difficult to sit still and I started to get a really bad feeling that I couldn't shake. To be quite honest, I don't remember much of that show or even how Pepper and

Chandi did – I'm sure they could sense I was distracted. I just remember being glad that Mum was there to see us perform and I treasured our time together.

A few weeks later, I mentioned to Mum in passing that there was a two-day show called All About Dogs taking place in May in Brentwood, Essex, and she was immediately encouraging.

'Well, I think you should all go – it would do you good. I'm doing all right and you'll only be gone for one night.'

I wasn't so sure. I'd watched her health change over the past few months and I was worried about leaving her alone for too long.

'Oh, I wouldn't go for both days, and it's too far to go there and back each day,' I replied.

She persisted. 'I think you should take your tent and stay overnight. It would be fun!'

I knew that Mum was still in pain, though she was doing a good job of trying to hide it from me, but with her encouragement I suddenly wondered if I really could go.

Mum sealed the deal by assuring me, 'If I need you, I promise I'll phone and you can come home.'

So it was decided. We were going to the show and camping as well, and I began to look forward to the prospect of another adventure with Pepper and Chandi. I gathered everything we needed, including a kettle and my tiny gas stove, purely so I could enjoy the luxury of a hot water bottle, as my feet get very cold at night. While I loaded the boot, the dogs milled about on the drive and kept trying to jump in the car, obviously keen to get on the road. We set off for Brentwood early on the Saturday in order to be there for the start of the show. Our first class wasn't until the afternoon, but I wanted to get there in plenty of time. The dogs were competing against each other in the same class, Pepper performing to a piece of tango music and Chandi to 'Walking the Dog'.

I expected that Chandi would be ranked higher than Pepper, so was surprised when the places were announced at the end of the class and Chandi was in second place with Pepper as the winner! I was extremely proud to have my two girls in the top two slots. We went up to collect our enormous trophy and, for the first time, prize money. It was a lovely and unexpected bonus – £50 for first place and £25 for second.

After our class had finished, we went back to the car and the dogs watched in anticipation as I erected the tent with apparent ease. I had given it a practice run on the lawn at home the day before to make sure that we would all have a roof, albeit flimsy, over our heads the following night.

By the time I'd put my mattress, pillows and duvet – yes, duvet: I hate sleeping bags with a passion – and the dog beds in the small two-man tent, it looked full but cosy. The huge silver trophy took pride of place at the back and I was so proud of Pepper for winning it.

After we'd eaten, we had a walk around the show-ground, which had now been transformed into a vast impromptu campsite, with dogs everywhere, all very well behaved for the most part. After our walk, it was quite late, and with another competition the next day, I decided to head back to the tent, fill my hot water bottle, settle down with Pepper and Chandi, and listen to the radio for a bit before going to sleep.

I lit the camping stove, having remembered to bring the matches, and filled the kettle with water before opening the boot of my car to find my hot water bottle – and then realized I had actually left it at home! I resigned myself to having feet like blocks of ice, but I was disappointed as I thought I had planned everything so well.

We all snuggled into our tent and the dogs went straight to sleep as they had had an exciting day. They always found it easy to drop off after a full day. I put the radio on and made sure that the air vent was open at the top of the tent. After a short while, I was nodding off too, so I turned the radio off and pulled the duvet around my ears, trying to ignore the cold biting my feet.

I must have just dropped off to sleep when Pepper turned over in her bed and kicked me straight in the face. Somewhat startled, I let out a muffled scream from under my duvet and, forgetting where I was, tried to stand up. My head met with a certain amount of resistance from the top of the tent, as it was nowhere near big enough to stand up in. Despite the commotion, Pepper and Chandi continued to snore very loudly, sound asleep. I extracted my head from the top of the tent and crawled back under my duvet.

The next time I woke up can't have been too much later. Chandi must have turned over in her bed and knocked her paws on the side of the tent as she rolled on her back, sending a shower of condensation all over my face. I awoke and sat bolt upright as the cold drops hit me and shouted, 'Oh shit! It's raining and the bloody tent's leaking!'

Both dogs were awake on hearing the S-word. They didn't like that word. It meant something was wrong, very, very wrong. I immediately wished with all my heart and soul that I hadn't said it, because they both desperately tried to sit on me in order to be as close and comforting as possible. As they moved, the whole tent shook and it felt as though someone had turned on a hosepipe as the large amount of condensation that had collected on the walls poured directly into my bed.

The night progressed in a similar manner – every time one of them turned over, I would get a soaking, and I wished that we could take it in turns to breathe in order to reduce the amount of condensation constantly showering me!

After a truly horrendous night, morning came and it was time to get ready for the second day of the competition. Again, both dogs were in the same class, and with some different competitors to the previous day, we were looking forward to the show. In spite of the very bad camping initiation we had all had, we once more collected prizes after the class finished. This time, Chandi was in first place, with her own matching huge trophy, and Pepper was in second place; again we received the same prize money. That weekend, we walked away with £150, two huge trophies and, most importantly, a resolution never to camp again.

The year continued and summer came and went. I didn't enter any more competitions, preferring instead to give Pepper and Chandi lots of lovely walks and continue with learning more new moves for our next routines without having to feel the pressure of an imminent competition.

Mum, of course, was constantly on my mind.

Now that the pain in Mum's hip had spread to her lower back, I helped her as much as she would let me by doing housework and lending a hand with the garden. Mum really hated needing to rely on me so much and was reluctant to let me help. It can't have been easy to feel her independence start to slip away. I made sure I was always there, though, when something was too much for her and she really couldn't manage.

Things took a turn for the worse just after Christmas 2002. The pain intensified and when Mum told me she was making an appointment with the doctor, I knew it was bad. Unfortunately Mum couldn't get an appointment with our usual GP, who knew her history and also had a strong interest in alternative medicine, so instead she saw a locum doctor. I went with her to the surgery and we were then sent up to the hospital to the orthopaedic clinic for a second opinion.

'What were you expecting to happen when you decided not to have treatment for your cancer?' the doctor asked Mum.

He told us the cancer had spread to her bones and all they could offer was palliative care. Mum had had her worst fears confirmed and it hit us both hard; he told us this was the beginning of the end.

Until the pain began in Mum's hip, she had enjoyed

nearly nine years of really good health. It had been her own brave decision to refuse conventional treatment and instead to pay attention to her diet and receive reflexology, healing and shiatsu treatments to try and hold the disease at bay for as long as possible. I fully supported and respected her choice, and that day, as I drove her home from the hospital, I promised her that I would be there for her and that she would stay at home where she belonged.

The next day, I took leave from my job at the school where I had worked part time, two mornings a week, for over eight years. The headmistress had agreed I could have a whole year off. I was going home to watch the person I loved most in the world fade away in front of my eyes.

Mum had liked to grow some of her own fruit and vegetables, but also bought produce from organic shops and for years had visited an organic nursery where you could pick your own fruit. It was there that Mum, Dad and I met Roy, the owner.

Roy was a shy but friendly middle-aged man with an attractive, weathered face and startling blue eyes. Mum and I became regular customers and would drive out to the peaceful nursery each week. We got to know Roy better and he became a good friend of ours. Roy is the kind of man who will stop and bend down to smell a flower. He loves animals and is extremely kind to all creatures, even the ones that inhabit his few acres of land and try to eat his carefully tended produce.

After Dad died, Mum and Roy became closer and they started going for walks together and taking trips to the seaside. It was lovely to see Mum happy and I was glad that she had someone who was good to her.

As Mum became more unwell, it became harder to travel, so Roy would regularly come over to see her. Chandi and Pepper both knew him well, so they were happy to have him around. When they first met, Pepper, in particular, had warmed to him instantly. She was a very good judge of character.

Roy was over for a visit one day when something happened to Mum. She had asked me to help her try an alternative therapy she had just heard about using caesium chloride. Taken correctly, it was supposed to kill cancer cells by making the body so alkaline that the cancer cells couldn't survive. I ordered some from America and also bought a quantity of potassium supplements, as caesium depletes potassium from the body and must be taken in conjunction with the right amount of potassium. Not doing so could be fatal.

Two days after beginning the treatment, on a Sunday afternoon in January, Roy had come to visit Mum, so

I went out for a walk with Pepper and Chandi. With Mum needing me more and more, and as I was still teaching a few afternoons a week from home, free time was limited and any I did have I spent with Pepper and Chandi. I didn't feel comfortable leaving Mum for long, so walks were shorter than usual, but neither dog complained. They just seemed happy to be with me when they could.

After our walk, I was taking advantage of a couple of hours to myself when I heard Roy shout up the stairs that Mum felt sick. What came next happened shockingly fast. After being sick several times, Mum started to have what looked very much like a seizure.

The paramedics came and got Mum into the ambulance. I told them about the caesium therapy and that Mum's symptoms were most likely caused by a potassium deficiency, but I'm not sure they believed me. There wasn't anything they could do at that stage anyway; it was their job just to keep Mum alive and get her to the hospital. By this time she was drifting in and out of consciousness. I went in the back of the ambulance and held Mum's head up. I was terrified of her choking on her own vomit. The ambulance had to reverse the entire length of the road we lived in, as somebody had parked their car in the turning area at the bottom of the cul-de-sac. Mum was hooked up to a heart monitor and it was going furiously fast – each time it started to speed up, she would pass out.

When we arrived, the doctors took Mum straight in and I was relieved when they decided to give her potassium. Before they had time to start a drip, however, Mum's heart stopped beating and I watched in horror as they resuscitated her in front of me. I remember feeling all the blood drain from my head and I started to fall to my knees. A nurse caught me and propped me up, and as she did, Mum's heart started to beat again. The doctor took me to one side a few minutes later and told me to prepare myself for Mum not making it through the night.

Roy had followed behind the ambulance in his car and was in the waiting room. I came out to tell him what was happening and asked if he would go back to our house and look after Pepper and Chandi. He left to look after the dogs for me and I could see how upset he was. I know he cared a lot for Mum. I didn't know how to comfort him, though.

Mum was transferred to the cardiac intensive care unit and I stayed with her through the night. It is a night I will never forget. One minute she would be talking to me, the next her heart would start to beat so fast she would pass out again. This happened so many times I lost count and we began to see it coming. She also needed to be resuscitated twice more during the night.

It was a strange night. When Mum was conscious, we were both so happy and for some reason even managed to find the whole dire situation funny. We were in absolute hysterics, with tears rolling down our faces. Then my tears would turn from joy to terror as her heart rate started to increase once more and we knew what was about to happen. We would look at each other and I would tell her I loved her. If these were to be the last words she heard me say, I wanted them to be that I loved her.

By morning, though, she was better and the potassium really started to take effect: her heart was beating normally again. I felt like death warmed up but was unbelievably glad that she had survived the night.

I stayed with Mum for the four days she had to remain in hospital and slept on the floor of her room. I would dash home twice a day to look after Pepper and Chandi, then go straight back to Mum. Somehow we all survived.

Mum was finally discharged and things settled down a little. When our lovely GP came out to visit Mum at home, he offered to help us try the caesium chloride treatment again; he could monitor Mum's blood potassium levels every day to be extra safe. But Mum was too frightened by the experience to try it again and so we left it there.

Winter turned into spring and then summer arrived, and was unrelentingly hot. It was extremely difficult to keep Mum cool and comfortable, and the noise of the fan drove her mad. She was in a lot of pain by this time and it would get worse suddenly, reaching unbearable levels, usually in the early afternoon and early hours of the morning.

Mum didn't want to take loads of painkillers, as she didn't want to dull her senses in the time she had left, so she put up with what seemed like an overwhelming amount of pain. I don't know how she did it, but I would sit with her until the pain lessened and do what I could to help. I was still using the Bowen Technique and it seemed to help a lot. I was just glad I could do something practical for her – I felt so damn useless and completely powerless the rest of the time.

Both Mum and I knew that she was dying, and for me, that was all there was in the world. I had taken a break from teaching my private students so I could care for Mum full time. I reached the point when I realized there wasn't any use fighting any more and I finally accepted the fact that I was going to lose her. There was nothing I could do to stop it happening. All I could do was be there, not leave her on her own, and just love her.

Pepper and Chandi didn't get a whole lot of my time that summer, but they both knew that things were very wrong, and whenever I had a few spare minutes, they would come and sit as close as they could, pressing their little faces into mine. I couldn't leave Mum in order to walk them and for many months they missed their usual exercise and outings. Fortunately, though, the lovely weather meant they could spend a lot of time quietly sitting or playing in the garden.

On several occasions I walked into the living room, where Mum now slept, to find either Pepper or Chandi just lying next to Mum's bed while she dozed, and one time they were both sat bolt upright next to the bed looking up at the ceiling. I have no idea what they were looking at, but it held their attention for the longest time.

To try and take my mind off Mum when I was trying to get to sleep at night, I started choreographing a routine in my head for Chandi, set to Ludovico Einaudi's hauntingly beautiful piece for solo piano, 'I Giorni'. I would think about it and start to visualize it in order to distract myself whenever I was feeling upset. I had been inspired by the idea of doing a routine dressed as a horse dressage rider and using the complicated dressage moves that Chandi already knew, as well as trying to teach her the passage move, a very elegant, high-stepping trot. She could already do perfect one tempis – our famous skipping move – and this dressage-themed routine would be the ultimate showcase for her talents, if it ever became reality. For now, it was just a fantasy, as my focus was very much on Mum.

*

One day in July, I received a Far infrared lamp in the post – I had read about their use for help with pain and had ordered one via the Internet. I set the lamp up and Mum tried it out. Amazingly, it really did help with the pain, but then of course the pain would return when the lamp was switched off. I suggested that we try to use it during the night as well. So that was the plan.

Six o'clock came and I had just given Pepper and Chandi their meat and bones for their tea when Pepper started to act peculiarly. My heart plummeted and I knew that something was very wrong. Pepper ran down the stairs and asked to go through the front door. We only used the front door when we were going to go in the car, so this was strange at this time of the evening.

I called Pepper to me and could see that she was repeatedly swallowing, as though she had something stuck in her throat. With only me in the house and Mum needing constant care, I really didn't know what to do. I called Roy in desperation and he came over and stayed with Mum while I took Pepper down to the nearest vet. I didn't want to spend time travelling the twenty-two miles to our usual holistic vet. This was an emergency. Chandi stayed behind, conscious that something was wrong, while I bundled Pepper into the car.

I'd rung in advance to say we were coming down, and when we arrived, I explained again that I thought Pepper had got a bone stuck in her throat. After a quick examination, to my surprise the vet concluded the bone had probably just scratched her throat. I tried to draw attention to Pepper's breathing.

'Can you hear that?'

'Hear what?' he replied.

'That raspy sound she's making when she breathes.'

He leaned in and listened closer. I was sure he must be able to hear it.

'No, I can't hear it.'

I wondered if he was going deaf; I could hear it so clearly.

I eventually realized that he wasn't going to believe me. He told me to bring her back in the morning if there was still a problem and I silently resolved to take Pepper to our usual vet. If we were waiting until morning, then I wanted her seen by someone we trusted.

That night went from bad to worse. Pepper was uncomfortable, Mum was in pain and I spent the whole night going from one room to the next worried out of my mind and trying to hold everything together. By 3 a.m., Pepper was asleep but dribbling profusely from the side of her mouth. I was even more certain that she had something lodged in her throat. Chandi spent the night curled up in her bed and didn't move at all. She was as good as gold and seemed to sense that I had a lot to deal with. I know my anxiety affected her, so I told her that everything was going to be all right, although at that point it felt as though everything was falling apart.

First thing the next morning, I rang my usual vet and she told us to come straight over. Roy kindly came over to be with Mum again.

Pepper had the most beautiful temperament, and despite her appalling treatment before she became mine, she trusted people implicitly and was calm and steady in any emergency. I stayed with her while she had her neck X-rayed, gently holding her so she didn't need to be sedated. As I suspected, there was a chicken bone lodged in her throat. When the X-ray revealed the size of the bone, the vet decided to anaesthetize her and attempt to reach it using forceps.

With Pepper unconscious on the operating table, the vet tried but was unable to reach the bone. I'd known that it wasn't going to go smoothly: we seemed to be all out of luck in our family. There was no choice but to make an incision in her neck into her throat. This was major surgery, and it absolutely terrified me. At almost nine years old, Pepper was no longer a young dog and any surgery involved a risk.

I waited outside while they carried out the procedure and then stayed with Pepper as she came round from the anaesthetic. A couple of hours later, I was allowed to take her home. I'd noticed a sizeable swelling on her neck over the incision, but the vet didn't mention anything about it and I had so much else going on in my head that I was just relieved that it was all over and that Pepper had come through the operation. I was glad that we could return to Mum.

When we got home, I settled Pepper in her bed in the small dining room next to Mum's room and offered her a drink. She drained the water bowl and wanted more, so I filled it up and put it by her and went next door to Mum. When I popped back in to see Pepper a few minutes later, the water bowl was empty again. I filled it back up, thinking it was peculiar, and went to get on with all the other things I needed to do.

A while later, I checked on Pepper again to find her staggering around the room with a confused expression on her face. My heart hit the floor – what was happening to her? I guided Pepper carefully towards the door, as when she tried to do it on her own, she bumped into the walls.

I took her outside so she could relieve herself and then brought her back in and let her drink more water before settling in bed. As I was stroking her, I realized the bedding was soaking wet and I thought that she must have spilt her water bowl. I was to discover an hour later, after I'd put her down clean and dry, that Pepper was wetting the bed and didn't seem to care. This was entirely out of character, as she was usually exceptionally clean. I knew something was terribly wrong.

For the next thirty days and nights, I had to take Pepper outside every forty minutes. I had to set my alarm to make myself get up. If I slept through the alarm due to sheer exhaustion, she would just wet her bed. As soon as Pepper had been outside, she would wobble to the water bowl and empty it once more, and so it continued.

Mum was in constant pain in the next room, and there were many times when I didn't know how to drag myself around. I was physically and mentally exhausted anyway, but this new development tested me to my limit. I kept saying to myself: What doesn't kill you makes you stronger.

By the third day, the lump on Pepper's neck had grown to the size of a large egg and started to ooze. I took Pepper back to the vet, who told me she had developed a haematoma and she needed yet another general anaesthetic to clean and re-stitch the opening. Apparently, bandaging the wound after the surgery could have prevented this and I wondered why it hadn't been done.

I wish the situation had been avoided and really didn't want Pepper to go under anaesthetic again, especially given what a poor state she was in. I asked the vet if she could do what needed to be done under a local anaesthetic and she was reluctant but agreed. However, if Pepper didn't keep still, she would have to knock her out completely. The vet had never done anything like this under a local before.

I'd had to leave Mum on her own this time, so I couldn't stay with my beloved Pepper, and it was with a very heavy heart that I left her at the vet's and Chandi and I drove home without her.

Even without me with her, Pepper stayed true to her beautiful self and let the wound be reopened, the huge haematoma be cleaned out and removed, and then the vet stitch her back up, all under local anaesthetic. The vet said that Pepper had looked up at her only once while she was cutting the stitches and then, once she had been reassured, just lay still and let her work.

I was so proud of Pepper and couldn't help but think what a different dog she was from the frightened scrap of a thing I'd taken home from the pound over eight years before. She was full of confidence and trust, and cast a spell over everyone with whom she came into contact.

By the beginning of August, Pepper had thankfully recovered, but Mum's condition had deteriorated. The cancer had spread further and it was now affecting the vision in her right eye, which made her feel really sick. I got some sunglasses and taped over the right lens so she was only seeing with her good eye, in the hope that it would help.

There were times each day when Mum would be talking to me and then suddenly pass out mid-conversation. She would be unconscious for anything up to half an hour at a time, and when she came to, she would have tremendous pain in her head. I would try not to let her see how terrified I was and each time I told her that everything was going to be OK; she was safe and I was there and wouldn't leave her. I was dying inside, though, and the fear that grew in me with each new symptom was crippling. I was dealing with all of this on my own and it was difficult. I was so grateful I had Pepper and Chandi with me.

One afternoon, Mum's friend Marlene drove up from Gloucester to see her. They'd met on a nursing course when they were seventeen and had been best friends ever since. I remembered meeting Marlene and her husband, Mike, when I was around ten years old and she had been a familiar face when I was growing up. Marlene used to come over regularly and visit Mum. Now that Mum was nearing the end of her life, Marlene would phone every day, and speak to me if Mum wasn't well enough to talk to her.

Mum was too poorly for Marlene to stay for long that day, and after they'd said their goodbyes for the very last time, I showed Marlene to the door.

She turned to me with tears in her eyes. 'I couldn't do what you're doing – I don't know how you're finding the strength to cope with all of this.'

I couldn't say anything, because I was so exhausted. I didn't know how I was doing it either.

For the final two weeks of her life, our GP, who was fantastic throughout Mum's illness, arranged for a Marie Curie nurse to come at night to give me a chance to get some sleep. I didn't sleep – I couldn't – but it was comforting to know that there was someone else in the house and I wasn't completely alone. Roy also came during the day and sometimes at night too, and it was only because of him that I was able to keep Mum at home, as I couldn't lift her on my own without hurting her, even though she was painfully thin by this time.

My mum finally left me at 7.14 a.m. on 23 August 2003, aged just sixty-four. I was at her side, as I had been throughout her illness. I had kept my promise that I would look after her so she could stay at home. A few days before she died, and during one of the last brief conversations we had while she was conscious, Mum had confessed that she'd thought I wouldn't be able to look after her and that I'd have to put her in a nursing home. At least I'd managed to show my mum that I was true to my word and proved my love for her in the only way I knew: by not failing her.

After she died, one of the Marie Curie nurses kindly dropped by to see me and brought a card. It read, 'I have never seen anyone care for someone else with such love and devotion, and I sincerely hope that you have some-one now to do the same for you.'

The truth was that I didn't have anyone close to me any more. What I did have was my beloved Pepper and Chandi, who were constantly by my side, sensing every one of my emotions and ready to comfort me in any way possible. They stayed with me at all times. I'm not sure what bad decisions I would have made if I hadn't had them to love me; the world was a very desolate and sad place, and I was floundering.

I had lost Dad just twenty-three months earlier, and Mum had suffered for nine months before disappearing in front of my eyes. Having lost both my parents to such painful ends, I was to spend the coming months drown-ing in grief. I would be driving the car or just walking down the street when I would suddenly have a flashback and be in the middle of everything, watching my mum cry out in pain. This would happen multiple times a day. It was so real I felt like I was reliving it all over and over again, and the tears would pour down my face. I would continue to have these flashbacks on a daily basis for around six years after Mum died, and would spend a long time slowly trying to achieve some kind of equilibrium in my life.

FIVE

Picking Up the Pieces

After Mum died, I was physically, emotionally and mentally drained. The only thing I wanted to do was take Pepper and Chandi out walking, so we would all pile into the car each morning and drive to Church Stretton and go up onto the Long Mynd, where we could walk, undisturbed, for as long as we wanted. One of our favourite walks took us to the highest point on the Mynd, called Pole Bank, where we could all sit down on the grass and enjoy the spectacular 360-degree view. It felt as though we had walked to the top of the world and the sheer beauty of the scenery all around us – patchwork-quilt farmland one way and majestic hills the other – somehow made me and my worries seem tiny in comparison. The many hours we spent there together, walking, playing and sitting, seemed to help put past events in perspective.

I loved watching the dogs excitedly running around

sniffing at all the interesting smells along the path. Occasionally Chandi would sneak up on Pepper and flip one of her long, hairy ears with her nose, which she knew annoyed Pepper and would make her give chase. Chandi would then scamper off immediately, looking over her shoulder at Pepper to check that she had had the desired effect. Pepper always rose to the bait and would charge after Chandi, her long tongue hanging out of the side of her mouth. Chandi would run like the clappers, twisting and turning, with Pepper close on her tail in hot pursuit.

Once Pepper had caught up with her, they would run side by side, playfully snapping at each other. At home, after they had finished chasing each other round the sofa and once the contents of their many toy boxes were strewn all over the floor, they would both lie down facing each other and roll onto their backs. They would then start snapping at one another and their teeth would bang together, looking and sounding rather like two crocodiles.

Spending so much time walking gave me lots of time to think about the events of the past two years and I had to be careful not to start to cry, because both dogs would race back to me with their ears down and such sad looks on their faces. They would try to jump up to lick the tears from my face. In the end, I would just sit on the ground and let them climb on me and lick me. They both loved me so much and were tuned into every change in my emotions. They were always there when I needed them and were my comfort and my joy.

Pepper would always do her best to get me to play with her. She would run off into the heather and search for a little twig to throw at my feet. She would lie down directly in front of me as I was walking, looking from the twig up to my face and back again. Chandi, seeing the fun Pepper was having, would find her own twig and they would take it in turns to have their twig thrown for them. It was impossible to ignore them and they always made me smile and helped me to forget my sadness.

I think it was at this time that I began to reassess my life and what I was doing with it. Up to that point, I'd been teaching, which was a job I'd never wanted to do. I used to think about how my life would have been different if I had gone to London and found work at a television company. I would never have adopted Pepper or Chandi for a start, and never known their unfaltering love and devotion, on which I had come to depend. Without realizing it, my outlook on life had been slowly changing since both dogs came into my life. I was aware that I used to be uptight, would worry about everything and was always disappointed if things weren't absolutely perfect. By being with my dogs all the time, though, I was able to watch the way they lived their lives – always happy and most importantly always living in the moment – and it had definitely rubbed off on me. Now I had stopped worrying so much, I was able to simply enjoy being with Pepper and Chandi every day. I would remember to be aware of the beauty around me, and it helped me to see that life was worth living. Each moment was perfect because I was with Pepper and Chandi, and they loved me.

Feeling the wind in my face and the sun on my back while the skylarks sang above our heads would make me very happy. Knowing that I had constant companionship and being so in tune with my two dogs was all I needed. We were a family, and I came to realize that family really does come in all shapes and sizes – and with varying amounts of fur.

Pepper and Chandi got me through those dark weeks and months immediately after Mum died. They comforted me and entertained me, even when I didn't feel like laughing; Pepper would persist with her antics until I did. Chandi would stick to me like glue, her little eyebrows knitted together in worry as she walked along looking up at my face. She knew how to make me forget my worries as well. I couldn't bear her to look sad, so I would have to cheer myself up and start to run around with them and have some fun.

I started teaching my private pupils from home again, but didn't feel well enough to go back to my school job straight away. In any case, as the headmistress had given me a whole year off, I still had another term in hand.

When I did return to school the following term, I was dismayed to hear that the headmistress would only be giving me five of the twenty pupils who had been mine. The children had been given a choice and, naturally, most had chosen to keep the temporary teacher they'd had during the year I was away. I wasn't prepared for this, but that was the situation I was facing and there was nothing I could do to change it.

I had to sell the house, as it was too painful being there and my income couldn't support the large bills. The prospect of going through all of Mum and Dad's personal belongings now they were dead was unbearable, but I knew that I had to and there was only me to do it, so I just had to get on with it. It was difficult and painful having to fold up all of Mum's clothes. Mum had already sorted all Dad's clothes after he died and put them in charity bags to give away. I had to keep telling myself that these were just 'things' and it didn't matter. Having lost my best friend, though, it was hard to think that way and I just wanted to cling on to everything. I couldn't imagine someone else wearing her clothes and walking in her shoes.

When I sorted through her old book cabinet, I found a box. I opened it up and inside seemed to be every birthday and Christmas card I'd ever given her. I opened the first card and looked at my childish handwriting. The words scrawled inside read:

> *Happy birthday, Mummy.*
> *Lots of love,*
> *Tina xxxxxxxxx*
> *P.S. I hope you're feeling better soon.*

After I'd read pretty much the same message in each card, I couldn't read any more. I placed the lid carefully back on the box and put it with the other things that I just couldn't bear the thought of throwing away.

The book cabinet, which had originally belonged to my maternal grandmother, had two doors with glass panels in them that opened up. I recalled that Mum had promised to buy me a proper cabinet to store the collection of mainly cut glass trophies Chandi, Pepper and I had amassed in competitions, complete with little lights to display them properly. Sadly, she didn't live long enough to fulfil that promise, but I had the idea of making the book cabinet into a display case for my trophies, and I felt suddenly that Mum would have approved.

When Roy, Mum's friend, rang me one evening to check if I was OK, I mentioned my idea to him and he came round the next day to see what needed to be done to 'turn it into the trophy cabinet of my dreams'. I really wasn't expecting him to make the adjustments to the cabinet himself, but he insisted. Knowing I didn't have anyone else to turn to, Roy would ring me every so often for a chat and he always said that if I needed anything, I should call him and he'd be there. I was so grateful for those kind words and they made me feel as though I wasn't completely alone.

After taking careful measurements, we went down to the DIY store to find some suitable small lights for the top of the cabinet. Roy went off to get pieces of glass and mirror cut for the shelves and back panel, and in the space of a day, he turned the old book cabinet into the best trophy cabinet I'd ever imagined. The cabinet, now completely full to bursting with Pepper and Chandi's trophies, takes pride of place in my living room.

As well as the cabinet, there was an old writing bureau of my grandmother's that I wanted to keep, and lots of old prints in quite ornate but somewhat faded gold-painted frames. I stored these pictures in the attic for many years, until one day I got them all down, refreshed the frames with some new gold paint and hung them in my living room. One print is of a young girl in a red dress holding a black long-haired puppy, with a red ribbon tied round its neck. This puppy reminds me of Pepper – it even has one of the same splodges of white under its chin. If it had the white mark above its nose as well, it would be the spitting image of how she would have looked as a young puppy.

After clearing and sorting out every room in the house, which took months, I made a start on the attic. I knew my parents kept the Christmas decorations up there and prepared myself to face all the memories they held. Christmas had been Mum's speciality and I would sit for hours making paper chains for Dad to hang from the ceiling. Mum would cook and bake vast quantities of goodies, and I could always expect loads of presents. I think Mum saved up all year to give me a good Christmas.

Mum had inherited an old container shaped like a hollowed-out tree trunk and painted to look like a tree covered in frost. I think it had originally held Christmas crackers and had belonged to my grandparents. It was the most enchanting thing. It came out every year and Mum used it to store a whole host of little presents.

It was always fun decorating the house together. I

adored the sparkly lights; in fact I've always had a fascination for any kind of lights, and if we ever went on a car journey at night-time when I was young, Mum would wake me up when we came near a town or a city so I could look at the hundreds of street lights. I have to confess to still being fascinated by them nowadays, and solar-powered fairy lights take pride of place in my garden so I can enjoy them every day of the year.

The Christmas tree, though artificial, took pride of place and would be laden with ornaments that Mum had when she was growing up. I loved listening to the stories she told each year about each one as we carefully lifted them out of their box. There was one little angel with gold wings that was wrapped like an Egyptian mummy in pink string. Mum always told me how she remembered her father wrapping this poor, naked angel with the string one year when Mum, as a little girl, was worried that it would be cold. I never met my mum's father, as he died after a series of brain haemorrhages at the age of fifty-two, when Mum was just twenty-one. All these ornaments had their own special place on the tree and were carefully looked after.

After Mum and Dad died, I couldn't face Christmas for a long while. What had been a lovely time with such wonderful childhood memories was now nothing more than an ordinary day, as there was no one to share it with. I know I was lucky to have my dad until I was twenty-nine, and my mum until I was thirty-one, but it has been so very hard being alone each year.

I always made sure that Pepper and Chandi had a fun day, though, and would fill two stockings full to bursting with presents for both of them. We would spend hours on Christmas morning playing with all their new toys. Then we would go for a walk. I'd put a potato in the oven to bake for my lunch, and once the dogs had in-haled their turkey dinner, we would fall asleep on the sofa, all cuddled up together.

When I finally made a start on the attic, as well as the box of Christmas decorations I found things that had been stored away up there for so long they'd been forgotten about. I spent days in the roof space going through every item in box after box, invariably crying as each item brought back fond memories. I kept the box of decorations and ornaments I took from my parents' attic, with all their treasured memories, but I still can't open it, even eight years later. It sits carefully packed away in my loft, along with other boxes of personal mementos I can't bear to open. Maybe one day I may be able to lift the lid, but I don't think it will be for many years to come.

Clearing the house was an enormous task and I thought I was never going to get through it. I did eventually manage to narrow it down to the things that

I just couldn't part with. Even then I was to find, much to my abject horror, that I had completely misjudged the amount of things I could stuff into my new home, a tiny two-bedroom house, which I moved into in February 2004, when the sale of my parents' house was finalized.

Our new end-of-terrace house, ten miles from Orchard House, was going to be a fresh start for me and the dogs, and I was glad when finally the trauma of moving was over, all the boxes were unpacked and we were settling in. The house was compact and had a small garden with enough room to grow a few vegetables and plant some fruit trees. I loved our new pad – I'd never had a house and my very own garden before, so it was fun planning all the things I was going to do with the place. The rooms inside needed some updating and I spent days stripping wallpaper and repainting the walls a soft vanilla colour, while Pepper and Chandi watched sleepily from the comfort of their beds after our long walks together.

I had bought the house because of its location. It was in a lovely position and I could see open fields from the upstairs windows. Only a few miles from Church Stretton, where we loved to walk, we were still able to go there frequently, but it also meant we were closer to another beautiful place we had been to before, Stapeley

Common, which has an ancient stone circle and magnificent views. It was extremely rare to meet other people and dogs when we were there, and that suited me – it was magical to have the place to ourselves.

With everything as close to normal as it was ever going to be, I immediately started to think about the Freestyle and Heelwork to Music competitions. The annual Rugby Dog Training Club competition was just around the corner. In my sadness I had briefly contemplated giving them up, but in the end decided to go in completely the opposite direction: I would throw my heart and soul into trying to produce the best routines ever with Pepper and Chandi.

With no time to lose, I sent off for the entry form for the Rugby show and set about coming up with ideas for routines. I decided that Pepper would do one more routine, which we would use for this show, and then retire from competition, as she was nearly eleven. I worked on choreographing a brand-new routine set to Harry Connick Jnr's 'It Had to Be You'.

Pepper had always enjoyed working on routines at home, but she was just as happy charging around in the bracken out on walks, enjoying her free time. I realized she wasn't going to miss competing and all the hours we spent perfecting routines. We would still practise her huge repertoire of tricks at home, but there would no longer be the pressure of competition hanging over us.

The dressage-themed routine for Chandi that I had begun to think about while Mum was ill was still just in its early stages. As yet, I hadn't had the time or inclination to start teaching Chandi all the other dressage moves we needed in order to make the routine as stunning as possible, so that routine was out of the question for this year's competition. I needed to come up with a different piece of music to work with. I was stumped as to what music to use until, watching TV one day, I heard a track that was just perfect for Chandi. It was Michael Ball's version of 'Me and My Shadow' and it was upbeat, energetic and lively – everything I wanted our next routine to be and the complete antithesis of how I was feeling.

As I listened to the song for the first time, I found I was choreographing it in my head and seeing the various moves fitting quite beautifully to the music. The song was easy to choreograph, with lots of words that Chandi could interpret with various moves and tricks that she already knew. We set to work on our new routines – I threw all my energy into them and Pepper and Chandi took up the challenge and gave it their best effort too. By the time the day of the show came around, we were ready.

This was the first public event I had been to since

losing Mum and Dad, and I was feeling very self-conscious and vulnerable. I wasn't even sure at that point whether I would have the nerve to go into the ring with everyone watching me and nobody there to support me, but I knew I couldn't let Pepper or Chandi down as they had both worked so hard on their new routines. I had to do it.

Pepper and I performed first, and together we gave a good performance, which helped to boost my confidence. Pepper held her head high and shook her beautiful locks at the crowd, lapping up the applause. With only a few minutes between the end of her performance and the start of Chandi's, we raced back to the car and I told Pepper how brilliant she had been on the way. As always, she had been marvellous in both spirit and performance. The routine turned out to be the best we had done together and was a great one to end Pepper's performing career.

I hurried to change my costume, warm Chandi up and get back into the hall ready to perform again. We made it in time and had a couple of minutes to collect ourselves before it was our turn in the ring.

Chandi looked at me intently as our names were announced: 'Please welcome into the ring Tina Humphrey and Bluecroft My Blue Heaven.' The audience started to clap and I asked Chandi if she was ready. Seeing her move into position close to my left leg, I took a deep breath and we made our way into the ring. Chandi was prancing by my side and I felt so proud watching her throw her legs high into the air on each step. I got the feeling that she was trying to reassure me by putting all her effort into her movements, and I was grateful.

We made our way to the centre of the ring and I nodded for the music to start. The atmosphere instantly changed in the hall, as it always did when it was our turn to perform. The constant murmur of conversation that had been a feature for most of the day completely stopped and the hall was silent.

No pressure, then, I thought.

The music started up and Chandi and I went through all the moves that we had carefully planned and practised. Everything was going well, although I still felt very nervous. I prepared myself to start the final section of the routine, which came after a slight pause in the music. The pause became a long break and then I realized the audience had started to clap. The DJ had stopped the music mid-routine, thinking we had finished.

Mortified and beginning to feel highly stressed, I had to walk over to the commentator and DJ and point out what he'd done. The commentator agreed it was the DJ's error and we were allowed to do the final missing section. After all the effort I had gone to with this routine and having pulled myself together enough to even make it to the show, I just couldn't shrug my shoulders and walk away!

A hundred times more self-conscious and nervous than before, I took my position on the floor again with Chandi, feeling like a real idiot while the DJ took an age to cue the music to the correct place. Chandi sensed my mood was starting to dampen. I bent down and whispered in her ear that everything was fine and she was please to try her hardest.

My little pep talk must have helped because Chandi finished the routine in style. We took our bows and galloped out of the ring back to where Pepper was waiting in the car. Chandi and I tied for first place in the end, but I confess I didn't enjoy that show one bit.

It was soon May again and time for the annual All About Dogs show in Essex. I decided we were ready for another adventure. Our previous wet camping experience hadn't given us the best memories, though, so I decided that this time we'd do it in style. Well, in a caravan rather than a tent! Dad had been really into caravanning and spent many summers driving us around when I was young. Mum wasn't as enthusiastic, but went along with it.

I was looking forward to using Dad's tiny Eriba Puck caravan, which he left me when he died. I disliked the bright orange curtains in the caravan, so set about making some shabby-chic red check ones as replacements, and with the matching duvet cover that I'd bought, the inside of the caravan looked really cosy. This is it, I thought: the adventure to top *all* adventures for the dogs and me!

When we got to the venue at Brentwood, we were told to wait for the tractor to help us onto the showground. As I'd never been to the show, or any show for that matter, with my caravan, I didn't think much of it. The tractor showed up and the driver attached a rope to the hook on the front of my car. What I soon realized was that Brentwood had experienced three weeks of non-stop rain and no one could get onto the showground without a tow from the tractor.

My heart sank as I realized the horror of the situation. There we were, dumped in the middle of what can only be described as a mud bath. I began to regret my decision to come, and I definitely regretted it once I'd opened the car door and gingerly put my foot down into the three inches of water that were sitting on top of the thick mud.

We were to stay for two nights this time and it was an absolute logistical nightmare trying to cope with Pepper and Chandi, whose legs got plastered with mud every time we stepped outside the tiny caravan. There was only enough floor space for one of them at a time. Thankfully,

I had loads of old towels in the back of the car, and after draping them over the seats, they could sit on them without covering them in mud (I hoped). It was impossible to get them clean or dry, and it was also terribly cold. The long fur on Pepper's legs absorbed everything and would take hours to dry. Once dry, we would have to go outside once more and the nightmare would start all over again.

I had been asked to judge several classes at this show, so the next morning, leaving the dogs in the caravan, I made my way to the large marquee where the competition was taking place. I was so cold and the thought of having to sit still and concentrate on routine after routine was not very appealing. Once the competition actually started, though, I watched each routine so carefully that I forgot about being miserable.

Everyone was somewhat subdued at that show, especially those of us unfortunate enough to be camping. Pepper and Chandi absolutely hated being covered in mud, as did I. Any areas of mud that we came across out on our walks at home they would carefully walk around, even if it meant having to go quite a distance to avoid getting their paws filthy. This must have been their worst nightmare come true. Thank goodness we weren't in a tent this time!

This was not the adventure we'd hoped for, and possibly the worst one we'd ever had, which is ironic as I'd been particularly looking forward to it. There was not a single minute that I remember fondly, and it was such a relief when we could finally be towed off the show-ground and were on our way back home. Just like the tent, I've never used the caravan again either!

Six

Moving in the Right Direction

With Pepper retired from competition but still very much enjoying training and practising her considerable repertoire of tricks at home, I now focused on trying to produce even better routines with Chandi.

The closing date for entries to the annual competition organized by Rugby Dog Training Club was just over three weeks before the event, but it didn't look as though we would be able to enter this year, 2005. It is against the rules to compete with a dog in season because it would be distracting for the other dogs competing, and Chandi was due at any time. It hadn't started yet, and if it didn't start soon, it wouldn't be finished before the event.

Two days before the closing date, feeling incredibly disappointed, I resigned myself to the fact that we would miss the competition. It was the tenth anniversary of the very first Heelwork to Music show held in the UK and it would take place in late February instead of April this year. Despite there being many different shows springing up each year, this was still the biggest and the best, and anyone who was anyone in the world of Heelwork to Music and Freestyle always showcased their latest routines there. Chandi and I were no exception.

The audience had been growing year on year, with representatives from the Kennel Club keenly watching the proceedings. Little did I know that this year there were to be more representatives at the show, as there was something in the pipeline that was to be announced in the days following the competition.

Somehow, luck was on our side and the very next day, only a day before the closing date, Chandi came into season, meaning that it would be finished just before the show. I scrambled to get the entry form in on time. As I really had thought that we wouldn't be able to go, I hadn't given any consideration to the two routines, Heelwork to Music and Freestyle, but I needed to include the musical tracks we were going to use on the entry form so they could be printed in the show's programme.

For the past few months we had been working a little on moves for the dressage-themed routine I had dreamed up while Mum was ill. I had already decided on the choice of music for this routine – 'I Giorni' by Ludovico Einaudi, a hauntingly beautiful contemporary piece for solo piano. We would use this for the Heel-work to Music class.

I had no idea what we were going to do for the Free-style event, though, so I needed to think fast. Just when I thought that I was never going to come up with anything, it occurred to me that if I was going to use a horse theme for the Heelwork class, then why not continue that theme for the Freestyle one as well and try to concoct a comedy showjumping routine? I racked my brains for horse-themed pieces of music that would be suitable and spent a whole afternoon going through my huge collection of records and CDs. I finally decided upon a combination of Mozart's 'A Musical Joke', the theme music from BBC's coverage of the Horse of the Year show, and the finale from Saint-Saëns's 'The Carnival of the Animals' – the power and speed of the music seemed to match the first tentative ideas I had in my head, and it felt right.

With the music choices finally sorted, and absolutely no time to waste, I hurriedly filled out the entry form and drove it down to the post office to make sure it got to the show secretary before the closing date.

We had three weeks to accomplish quite a daunt-ing task. Firstly, I had to choreograph just over eight minutes of routines, then rehearse and perfect them both with Chandi. Usually one routine takes us about five months. With time against us, I was going to have to work fast. Chandi and I had our good reputation to uphold and there was no way that I was prepared to be at the show with a routine that was anything but perfect.

We were struggling a little with the passage move, which can be described as a highly elevated and extremely powerful trot, for the Heelwork to Music class. That description perhaps doesn't do the beauty of the movement justice – it truly looks as though the horse, or in this case my beautiful, elegant Chandi, is floating on air.

Once Chandi was into the movement, I could get her to lift her legs by repeating the sound 'tuh, tuh, tuh, tuh', gradually increasing the speed of my delivery. I didn't stop to think about the mechanics of why this worked, but it was highly effective and seemed to really encourage her. I was to discover a couple of years later exactly why this worked, but for now it was something that I just did instinctively.

After a couple of days of intensive effort, the passage move was starting to come together. Chandi was still having trouble going directly into the movement from a standstill, but we kept working and I could see signs of progress. I then began working with her for a few seconds at a time when we were all out walking, calling Chandi to me and asking her for a few steps of passage.

Little and often was going to be the key, with time well and truly against us.

For the Freestyle showjumping routine to be really impressive, we needed to use a showjump. Using a prop immediately opens up a whole array of different moves, as Chandi and I have an object with which to interact. In previous years, we had only ever used a dance cane to work with, but this was going to be different and really set the scene for the routine. I sat quietly and tried to imagine all the things we could do with the jump, apart from the obvious thing – jumping over it.

The more I let my imagination run riot, the more I started to like what I was seeing in my mind's eye and the story behind the whole routine started to develop. I saw this Freestyle routine as being the complete opposite to the serious, emotionally charged Heelwork to Music routine, which demanded perfectly executed movements, with changes of pace from walk to passage to one tempis, where Chandi skips, and so on. The intricacy of movement that I was planning for this routine was like nothing we, or indeed anyone else, had done before, and with the correct music, and a beautiful theme, I knew we were working on something really special. The goosebumps I got whenever I thought of it let me know, as they always did, when something was just right.

With the moves for the Freestyle routine developing

try even harder on subsequent attempts. My movements and Chandi's movements were identical and it was crucial that they matched precisely. Just one tiny mistake would be instantly obvious and spoil the intricate nature of the routine and everything I was trying to create.

I made the decision to do the entire routine with my hands held neatly behind my back, to show that Chandi was undeniably performing entirely from verbal cues. The first time I tried the movements on my own, with my hands held in this position, it felt right. Chandi was already working from verbal cues, as I really disliked giving hand gestures to encourage her into the various positions.

This meant that Chandi had to concentrate and listen to every quietly uttered word from me. The breadth of her vocabulary is enormous and so is her ability to focus 100 per cent, even under the unique and tense atmosphere of a competition.

Meanwhile, the Freestyle routine was coming along nicely and the moves for that were also starting to take shape. I had taught Chandi many ways of 'avoiding' jumping the jump. For example, she learned to approach the jump and, instead of leaping over, crawl under it and then crawl backwards under it to rejoin me. I'd also taught her to approach the jump while she was between my knees, so it looked like I was riding her like a tiny horse. All of these individual moves and sequences had been learned by practising numerous times throughout the day in the living room. Now finally the time had come when we needed to put each move together as a whole and see how my ideas would work as complete routines.

I always dread doing a routine all the way through for the very first time, and this was no exception. However, unless I'd misjudged everything and made a serious mistake with the choreography, I knew from past experience that with each subsequent attempt, the moves would start to take shape fairly quickly.

It was early February and bitterly cold. We have a special place up on the Long Mynd where we rehearse complete routines. I've always used this same spot, as it is never waterlogged, despite any amount of rain, is accessible by car, allowing easy transportation of various props, and is relatively flat. The only problem with it is that when it is cold, it is freezing and terribly exposed. So many times we have worked there in such strong winds and driving rain that we can barely stand up. The effort and sheer struggle during some of our practice sessions always makes performing indoors at the competition, on a completely flat surface, seem easy by comparison.

Chandi doesn't like being cold, so I make sure that we always have the heater on full blast in the car on our journey, and that she is wearing a couple of layers of coats that we can peel off as she warms up. She is always keen

Tina, aged nine, riding Mr Jinks at her first riding lesson.

Chandie, the family Labrador, 'flying high' over a favourite jump.

Tina, aged fourteen, with Chandie.

Chandie with Tina's parents, Diane and Brian.

Tina, aged seventeen, on *Jim'll Fix It* playing Gershwin's 'I Got Rhythm' with Jonathan Cohen.

Chandie, the family Labrador, and Pepper, aged one year, in Orchard House garden.

Tina and Pepper, before their first Crufts performance in 1999.

Chandi, aged four months, two days after bringing her home from the pound.

Chandi and Pepper at their first *Dogs Today* photoshoot.

Pepper, aged eleven years, snuggled in her bed – note the relaxed tongue!

Chandi practising the famous ballet routine on the Long Mynd, Shropshire.

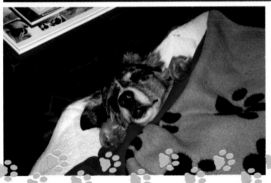

Tina and Chandi on the podium after winning the Crufts International Freestyle Final, 2009.

Chandi tucked up in bed.

Tina and Chandi at the annual Coventry show,
performing their famous back-to-back move.

Chandi modelling her favourite
Chandana for our online shop
www.chandana-heaven.com

Chandi on her twelfth birthday with
her favourite new toy.

Tina and Chandi at the *Britain's Got Talent* semi-final.

Tina and Chandi at the final.

Chandi showing me a tree.

Chandi enjoying celebrity life.

Chandi enjoying an
Autumn adventure.

to get started, remembering, I think, that soon enough she will start to get warm, as she uses her athletic body to the fullest extent possible. What we both battle against during training builds our stamina and powers of concentration. I don't think training in a nice, warm indoor area would be anywhere near as satisfying for us.

With Pepper tucked up under her fleecy blanket in the warmth of the car, Chandi and I braved the cold and started to warm up, trying out heelwork in different directions and then adding more circles, followed by backwards movements to ensure her muscles were nice and warm before we attempted our first run-through.

With our portable CD player ready and waiting, I pressed play and quickly got into position with Chandi by my side for the first complete run-through of the dressage routine. The music began and off we went.

Right from the start, everything went wrong. The movements didn't fit with the music and we were dreadfully out of time. I kept treading on Chandi's paws and she tripped me up a few times, but we continued right through to the end. We stood and looked at each other when the music finished and both gave a huge sigh. I could see the tension in her forehead, causing her little eyebrows to almost knit together. Her ears were back and flat on her head. It felt like a total disaster, but we weren't going to give up that easily.

I went over to the CD player and pressed play once more, calling Chandi into position. The music started and off we went again. This run-through went better and more of the movements fit with the music. I managed not to step on Chandi's paws this time, and she managed not to trip me up. We were both pleased and felt more confident. It hadn't been perfect, but it was definitely taking shape! We tried it once more and then worked on the individual moves that needed more practice.

At the end of the session, we were both out of breath with effort, but I could tell Chandi was pleased by the keen expression on her face. Her ears were standing bolt upright on her head and she was looking up at me, her mouth cracked open in a huge grin. This was her eager and relaxed expression, and I much preferred to see her looking up at me like this rather than the way she had looked at me after the first awful attempt.

The routine was over four minutes long and was completely exhausting for both of us. It may not sound like a great deal of time, but the level of concentration needed is extremely high and it can really take it out of you.

After the practice, we packed the CD player away and went for a walk with Pepper to wind down. The next day, we would return to run through the showjumping routine. Based on our dressage run-through, I was confident that after a few attempts, the Freestyle routine would take shape just as quickly, so I tried to stop thinking about it for now.

We were up against the wire getting these two routines together in only three weeks, but unbelievably we were on course and rehearsed the routines three or four times each day.

With five days to go, everything so far had been going well. Our luck was about to change, though, as we had heavy snow overnight, which meant our training ground was completely inaccessible. The closest place we could find that was big enough to train was also under a good foot of snow and had a definite slope to the left, but we would just have to manage.

Getting out of the comfortable, warm car only to be hit by the bitterly cold wind was something I dreaded at the start of every training session, and on this occasion I really needed to psych myself up even to open the car door. We carried on regardless, though, wrapped up in coats, trotting, skipping and dancing through the deep snow. Huge snowflakes fell all around us and we were both caught up in this magical shared experience.

I think of Chandi as my equal; we are a true partnership in everything we do. She understands when we are working on a new routine and realizes that by the time we are doing complete perfect run-throughs, the day of a performance is imminent.

Working on a routine with Chandi makes me completely happy and fulfilled. There isn't anything else in the world but the two of us and all my problems just fade away. Looking into her beautiful brown eyes as she eagerly gazes up at me while we go through the moves is enchanting, and the connection that I feel to her is more than I ever imagined possible.

The best way I can describe what we create is sheer, unadulterated magic. I can feel the energy whizzing backwards and forwards between the two of us as we work together. If anything ever distracts us mid-routine, it is a horrible feeling – like suddenly crashing down to earth or being slapped in the face, and we become just a person and a dog again. The magic is shattered.

We both need to be completely focused on each other the entire time to create the routines we do. Chandi hates being interrupted while she's working with me and this is the only time that she will bark aggressively, other than when someone knocks on the door of our house. Time and time again Chandi shows the same dedication to events that I do, and her intelligence and commitment to her work are immense.

Finally the day of the show arrived, and we were ready. With the showjump safely packed into the boot of the car and my two costumes neatly hanging in their covers to keep them clean, we set off for the show. I have a habit of playing the tracks I'm using for our routines over and over again as I drive, thinking through every movement and command and saying them out loud. After raising her head once as she heard me say, 'Ready, trot,' Chandi settled back down to sleep. I needed to focus on the routines and run them through in my mind as many times as I could. It was a lot to remember and my worst nightmare would be to forget the routine as we were performing.

Our two classes weren't until the afternoon, which meant I had plenty of time to wonder how our new routines were going to be received by the huge audience. No one had seen them but me, and I had only seen them from my unique vantage point – working next to Chandi. I didn't know what the audience was going to see or whether it was going to be as effective as I imagined. All I could do was have faith in the imagination that had produced the routines and enjoy being in the ring with Chandi.

After bringing the showjump into the hall ready for the Freestyle class, I changed into my beautiful and very expensive dressage costume. Chandi was excited to be at the show, and as I lifted her out of the car and placed her gently on the ground, she opened her nostrils really wide to take in all the new smells. I had walked Pepper around the exercise area already so she could stretch her legs, and she had happily jumped back into the relative warmth of the car, where she would snooze while Chandi and I performed.

Chandi was keen to start work and we warmed up outside with some stretching, circling moves and then some trotting and cantering in all directions. We returned to the car, grabbed the water bowl and the small pot of cheese I kept for her reward after a performance and told Pepper, who was now contentedly snuggled under a fleecy blanket, that we wouldn't be long.

Chandi and I went round to the entrance of the hall and walked in. We still had about fifteen minutes to wait before it was our turn in the Heelwork to Music class, so I walked her round to keep her muscles warm and left her coat on until it was almost time for us to go into the ring.

Our routines don't start once we're in the ring; I decided a long time ago that our routines start outside the ring and we walk in together fully focused and in character. We practise the walk in and the bow to the judges in acknowledgement when we are preparing the whole routine at home, so everything seems comfortable and familiar.

I felt the magic begin between me and Chandi the second the music started. Completely absorbed in the routine, at one point I was back on the hill with the snowflakes dancing in the air around us. I was transported to the most magical place where again only Chandi and I existed. The hall was silent and you could literally have heard a pin drop. All eyes were on us, watching and analysing our every move.

We got to the Spanish Walk, another advanced dressage movement where Chandi lifts and stretches out each front leg in turn. To show us working in harmony, I extended my legs, too, synchronising our movements in time with the music. Every movement was perfect until one where Chandi lowered her leg a fraction too soon. It didn't matter, though, and we moved on to the next section with its beautiful passage and one tempis, and then into our breathtaking back-to-back move.

The last section went smoothly and then we were taking our final bow to each other as the music stopped. It was all over. There was a brief silence in the hall, and then the applause started. Chandi started to run round me when she heard the audience's reaction and her whole body was wagging from side to side in excitement. I always applaud her myself during training as I simultaneously praise her for a job well done. I started doing this to get her used to hearing that kind of noise, but she now regards the sound of applause as praise in its own right, so having this many people all clapping feels to her like a massive reward. I think she knew that together we had just created something incredibly beautiful.

When I was putting this routine together, I had no idea of the background to the music. I discovered later that the inspiration for 'I Giorni' came from a twelfth-century folk song from Mali about a hippopotamus that was cherished by the residents of a nearby village but killed by a hunter. The song is a lament for the death of a king or a great person, or for the loss of a loved one. It was fitting, then, that I had dedicated this routine to Mum. I like to believe that Mum and Dad were in the front row watching us that day.

Chandi and I didn't have much time before we were due back in the ring for the next class. We didn't even have time to wait to hear our scores being announced. I grabbed the pot of cheese and gave Chandi a few pieces to say thank you and well done. After a quick slurp out of the water bowl – Chandi, not me – we went out to the car to say hello to Pepper and change my jacket.

We got back to the hall a few minutes before we were due in for our Freestyle routine, and as I'd again warmed Chandi up outside, I kept her walking round for a few minutes inside and then asked her to lie down in the corner while I went to fetch the showjump from the side of the hall.

When it was our turn, a member of Rugby Dog

Training Club helped me carry in the jump. I needed to position it in exactly the right place and I took my time. If I got it wrong, when Chandi came to do her final move there was a real danger of her not having enough room to clear the jump, and if placed at the wrong angle, she could land on the judges' table.

With the jump in position, I walked out of the ring to collect Chandi, who had been patiently waiting and watching my every move. As always, she pranced into the ring with me, and when we reached our opening position, I bent down, wished her luck and kissed the top of her head.

I nodded for the music to start and we were off! The opening moves went well and there was a slight murmur of laughter from the audience. We continued as we had planned and reached the point where Chandi grabbed the pole and ran off with it, leaving me to chase after her. I was aware of a roar of laughter from the audience and was pleased, but I didn't have time to dwell on it for more than a millisecond as Chandi and I had to keep concentrating. I couldn't afford to get distracted, as the result would be disastrous. I have on several previous occasions forgotten a routine while performing and it is exceptionally scary. Each time that has happened, Chandi has saved the day by just continuing with the next move, cueing me as to which move comes next.

No such incidents today, though: everything was going well. We were nearing the big finale – the hops on her hind legs towards the jump, then the gallop and the final leap over it. As soon as Chandi cleared the jump, I punched the air with my fist to show my delight at finally managing to get my 'naughty pony' over the jump. The audience cheered and clapped as Chandi and I bowed to all four sides of the arena.

As I had to take the showjump back out to the car, I collected it up there and then, after giving Chandi some more cheese. We were in the hall to hear our scores this time, though. We had gone into the lead! There were still, however, some more teams left to compete and I had no idea whether we would hold on to our current place. We returned to the car and started to pack everything away so we would be ready to leave the show as soon as the results were announced and the prize-giving had taken place.

Getting back to the car, Pepper wagged her tail, pleased to see us, and Chandi leaned forward to sniff noses with her in greeting. I let Pepper out of the car for a run around. Soon she was asking to return to the warmth of the car, so Chandi and I made our way back into the hall to see how we had done at this special tenth-anniversary show.

The results for the Heelwork class were announced

in reverse order, with each handler and dog going into the ring to collect their rosette when they were called. When it got to the second-place team being announced and we were the only team still left outside the ring, I knew we'd won the class with our dressage routine! After having photographs taken with our beautiful cut-glass trophy and red rosette, we were all sent out of the ring so the results of the Freestyle class could be announced, again in reverse order. I held my breath and chewed my lip, while Chandi sat unperturbed by my side.

I knew at one point we had been in the lead. But had we held on to it, or had someone else beaten us to the trophy? Everything seemed to happen in slow motion from that point on and it took an age for second place to be announced. It wasn't us! We had won the Freestyle class as well!

Chandi was the first, and is still the only, dog to have won both Heelwork to Music and Freestyle classes on the same day at this show and I was so proud of the effort that she put in to achieve so much in such a short amount of time. I suddenly thought about how just three weeks ago, these routines didn't exist, and a wave of exhaustion and relief washed over me.

For the first time I was completely delighted with our routines and couldn't fault them. I had finally figured out how to translate the ideas from my imagination into routines that worked in reality and propelled us to the very top of each discipline. Chandi wasn't just the best Heelwork to Music dog in the country, she was the top Freestyle dog too, and we had just set our first record by winning both classes!

Once someone had uploaded the video footage to YouTube, our routines attracted the attention of tens of thousands of people around the world. For weeks the video received between 30,000 and 40,000 hits a day, and the feedback and comments that were left on our own website were beautiful and moving to read. Nearly every one talked about the obvious love and devotion between Chandi and me when we performed.

SEVEN

Chandi Plays her Part
to Perfection

A few days after our double success at the show, there was a very exciting announcement in the world of Freestyle and Heelwork to Music. For the very first time, there was going to be an official combined Heelwork to Music and Freestyle competition at Crufts that same year! It was to be an invitation-only event, with only the top ten handlers and dogs invited to take part. Chandi and I had been looking forward to taking the rest of the year off from competing, so this announcement came as a huge surprise to me.

In 2003, Heelwork to Music and Freestyle had become an official Kennel Club-registered canine sport, but I hadn't seen the significance of this new development at the time. What I didn't realize was that my beloved sports were now on equal footing with the other long-recognized sports of agility, flyball and competitive obedience, and shows were being run under official Kennel Club rules and regulations.

The shows we had entered over the years had been called 'demonstration events', but this recognition meant that both Heelwork to Music and Freestyle could be included for the first time as an official competition at Crufts. Like so many other dog enthusiasts, for me it was a dream to be able to compete in our discipline at the biggest dog show in the world. Pepper, Chandi and I had previously performed at Crufts, in the special events ring, but this time things were very different – we could now compete officially and in the top ten of our chosen sport!

The online forums buzzed with excitement as people began to receive their invites and I eagerly awaited ours – I was certain Chandi would be one of the ten entrants after our double success a few weeks before. When a week passed by with no sign of a letter, I emailed the Kennel Club to politely remind them of our track record. I didn't get a reply, but the next day I received an invitation by email, and that was good enough for me. We were going to Crufts to compete!

Since Crufts wasn't for another five weeks, there was time to give Chandi a break before practising for the competition. For the combined Heelwork to Music and

Freestyle competition, we would only need to perform one routine, so we chose our latest showjumping-themed Freestyle routine.

With a serious amount of equipment to get into the NEC in Birmingham, I realized I was not going to be able to manage on my own. I phoned Roy to ask if he would mind coming along to the show to help me transport everything into the hall. Roy had not previously been involved in any of our competitions, but now neither Mum nor Dad was around to come with me, I hoped he would be a friendly face with whom to share the experience. He kindly agreed and added that he was looking forward to it.

The day of the competition dawned, and having organized everything I needed to take the night before and carefully packed it in the car, Pepper, Chandi and I were ready to set off as soon as Roy arrived. As arranged, bang on the dot of 5.15 a.m., Roy rolled onto my driveway, bringing his sack truck trolley with him to help move the equipment. We transferred it to my car and off we went.

The journey to the NEC only took around an hour and a half and we arrived in the car park in good time. I unloaded the car, piling everything onto the tarmac, and Roy tied it all to the trolley so it wouldn't fall off as we made our way into the show. After much laughter and wobbling as we tested its balance, Roy pulled the heavily laden trolley and I carried a bag full of everything that wouldn't fit on it. I held Pepper and Chandi's leads with my other hand. We made our way through the car park in the freezing wind with hundreds of other people and dogs. I was so thankful to Roy for helping me, as I don't know how I could possibly have managed on my own.

When we reached the cramped hall next to the special events ring, I found our allocated bench. There was a laminated card with my name on it – my surname was spelled wrong, but it was exciting to see it with the Crufts logo all the same. We unpacked the trolley and I made the dogs comfortable.

The noise was deafening in the hall and there was barely any room to move as there were so many people milling about and spilling off the trade stands next to the benching area. The atmosphere was good, though, with a definite air of excitement.

This was a momentous day for Chandi and me, and for the sport. The inaugural combined Heelwork to Music and Freestyle competition was starting shortly and there was already a huge queue of people waiting to get a seat in the stands, arranged on all four sides of the special events ring.

We had arrived early so I could show Chandi the ring she would be performing in before the programme of events started. Leaving Pepper in Roy's care, Chandi and

I went to take a look. Many of the other competitors, all of whom I knew from previous shows, were already in the ring throwing toys for their dogs to chase and doing warm-ups.

We paused at the entrance to the arena. Chandi was by my side looking around at all the activity, and as I gently touched the side of her face, she turned to look up at me. I nodded, smiled and asked, 'Are you ready?'

Chandi winked at me and I laughed.

'Come on, then,' I said, and side by side we trotted into the ring and onto the AstroTurf.

We both paused again and I felt a rush of emotion. I was excited, nervous and incredibly proud of us. I crouched down next to Chandi, cupped her face in my hands and looked deep into her eyes.

'I love you, Chandi, and I'm so proud of you,' I told her.

Chandi wriggled forward, put her front paw on my arm, curling her toes so she was holding me, and licked the side of my face.

'Right,' I said, standing up, 'let's have a crack at some heelwork, shall we?'

Chandi's eyes shone as she looked at me and pricked up her ears, telling me she wanted to do some work. We both knew this was a huge occasion, and as we moved forward, Chandi pranced and strutted beautifully next to me, doing perfect heelwork.

We weaved our way around the other handlers and dogs in the ring, and Chandi focused all her attention on me. She wasn't distracted by the lights, the music, which suddenly blasted out over the public address system, or the other dogs charging around the ring.

Chandi and I spent a few minutes working in the ring and then we made our way through the crowds back to Roy and Pepper. Chandi jumped up next to Pepper on the bench and lay down on her bed. There was no likelihood of her having a snooze, as she was too excited by everything that was going on around her, but with the thick blanket I had draped over the top, the dogs at least had some privacy and felt safe.

The competition was due to start around 10.30 a.m., and Chandi and I had been drawn ninth out of the ten competitors, which is a great position to have in the running order, but it meant that we had an agonizing hour-long wait until it was our turn on the famous Crufts 'green carpet'.

I changed into my costume, and eventually our competition was announced and the first competitor entered the ring. I focused on what I had to do and tried not to pay attention to anything else. Once I heard competitor number seven being announced, it was time to get Chandi warmed up so she would be nice and supple before our turn in the ring.

I'd sent Roy off ages ago to get a seat in the arena to watch the competition, and he hadn't come back, so I presumed that he'd been lucky. Chandi and I said good-bye to Pepper, who would wait for us on the bench, and made our way through the crowds of people to the collecting ring and saw that our showjump was still safely tucked away in the corner where I'd left it. One of the stewards came over and asked where I wanted the jump set up in the ring and I explained where to put it.

During the short delay while the scores were being decided for the previous competitor, the showjump was taken in and I watched to make sure it was put in the correct place. This ring was vastly bigger than the one at the Coventry show, but I still needed the jump to be at the right angle so the three judges, who were sat behind a table on one side of the ring, could clearly see all our moves and so we weren't hidden behind the jump.

The eighth competitor was still in the collecting ring waiting to hear her scores, but as soon as they were announced, it was time for Chandi and me to walk out in front of the huge audience.

'This is it, kid,' I said.

Chandi wagged her tail in reply, and we both headed into the ring. Once we reached our starting position,

I settled my mum's old riding hat firmly on my head and nodded for the music to start. When Chandi saw that cue, I felt her adjust her position next to my leg in anticipation.

The audience had obviously been well warmed up, as they were very loud and appreciative whenever Chandi did anything super clever and funny. The reaction from the crowd encouraged us both and lifted our performance. We thoroughly enjoyed ourselves in the limelight, and the applause delighted Chandi! She had a huge grin on her face and was keenly working her way through all the different moves and tricks in our routine.

We were coming up to the final sequence of difficult moves where Chandi was to run through my knees and then immediately go up on her hind legs. As she ran forward, though, I was almost knocked off balance as she misjudged the space, went too close to my leg and whacked the side of her head on my knee. Chandi gave a half-shake of her head and I gasped, forgetting to cue her to go up on her hind legs. Without so much as a pause, and proving once more how much she loves performing, Chandi stood up on her back legs and bounced along four times before galloping towards the jump and clearing it with feet to spare.

Our big finale delighted the audience and they roared and clapped when Chandi finally cleared the jump. After bowing to the audience on all four sides, we ran out together and back into the collecting ring.

Chandi wagged her tail so hard that her whole body moved, and I told her how clever she was. We had gone into the lead in the competition! With only one competitor left to perform, I took Chandi back to the bench to give her a drink of water and check in with Pepper, who was patiently waiting for us to return.

I could hear the music for the tenth and final routine playing in the ring coming to a climax and the audience's reaction seemed very enthusiastic. I held on to Chandi as I waited for the scores. There was a long pause before they were announced. They were very high and I was suddenly sure that our competitors must have taken the lead.

It seemed like an age before I knew how we'd done. The benches were adjacent to the performance ring and we could hear the commentator's voice booming over the tannoy as he talked a little about some of the routines that had just been performed and encouraged the audience to show their appreciation for all the competitors.

As I glanced quickly down the row of benches, I could see the nine other competitors stood with their dogs, waiting, as I was, to hear the final result. The three judges counted up their scores for content, accuracy and musical interpretation, verifying each one to make sure no mistakes had been made. Building up the tension in the ring, the commentator was making us all wait.

Then suddenly I heard him announce, 'The winners of the first Heelwork to Music and Freestyle competition are . . . Tina Humphrey and Bluecroft My Blue Heaven!'

As the audience cheered and clapped, I spontaneously burst into tears. I'd been convinced that we hadn't won, but we had done it after all; we had won the inaugural Crufts Heelwork to Music and Freestyle competition! Chandi, my rescue dog, had proved herself repeatedly to be the best in the country and I was overwhelmed.

Chandi and I went back into the ring with all the other competitors and dogs for the awards ceremony. As usual the places were announced in reverse order, and one by one the dogs and handlers went to shake hands with the judges and collect their rosettes.

Chandi and I were presented with the prize for first place, a beautiful crystal vase engraved with the Crufts logo and the details of the competition. As we stepped forward, the audience applauded enthusiastically, and while my heart filled with pride, my eyes once more filled with tears. I wished that my mum had been here to witness this moment and share in the successful realization of a cherished dream. I reached out to shake hands with the judges and was then handed our trophy and rosette. I showed Chandi the extravagant three-tier Crufts green rosette for first place. She reached out and grabbed one of the ribbons in her mouth; she wanted to hold her rosette, so I let her.

Photographs were then taken of the top three handlers and dogs crouching down in front, with the three judges lined up behind. I have the photo hanging on my landing; the two other dogs are looking at the camera, but Chandi has both front paws on me, looking straight into my eyes. I knew that if she could speak, she'd be saying, 'We did it, Mum! We did it!'

The competition was over, but our day was not finished. As the winners, Chandi and I had to perform our routine once more, much later in the day. After our second performance, Roy and I sorted out all our kit and once more lashed it to the trusty trolley to make the long journey back to the car park. Roy was delighted that we had done so well in the competition and said that he was really glad he had been there to witness our success. I made sure that the crystal trophy, which was safely packed into its box, was in no danger of getting broken. This trophy was going to take pride of place in the display cabinet at home.

It was lovely having someone to talk to about the day's unique events as we travelled the hour and a half back home in the dark that evening. It had been a long and exhausting day. I'd been up since 4.15 a.m. and I was shattered. But just as I had always done with Mum after one of my concerts when I was a child, Roy and I talked about every detail over and over again, and I forgot how tired I was as we chatted away while I drove steadily home, Pepper and Chandi contentedly asleep on the back seat.

I listened intently as Roy told me about his favourite moments of the routine and the great reactions of the audience around him. Roy told me he thought Chandi and I had been fantastic and that the routine was brilliant. It was lovely having him there, but it made me miss Mum all the more.

When we'd finally got home and unloaded the car, and I'd waved Roy off, I was so tired I could barely keep my eyes open. I prepared the dogs' food and grabbed just an apple and a piece of cheese for myself. Then we all headed upstairs for bed.

That night is the only night Chandi has got on my bed without asking permission. Usually, Chandi slept in her own bed, by Pepper's, both beds next to mine, but that night was different. I opened the door to the bedroom and was surprised to see her curled up on my bed with her head nestled in the centre of my pillow. When she saw me, she gave the biggest sigh and closed her eyes. We slept side by side that night.

The next morning, Chandi woke me by placing her

cold, wet nose in my ear. With a jolt I opened my eyes to see her flop back down onto the bed with her chest and front legs on top of my legs.

'Right!' I threatened in mock anger. 'I'm going to bounce you up and down!' and I started to raise and lower her with my knees until she was bouncing around on the bed. After a couple of bounces, her mouth opened and she started to make a curious noise like irregular panting, though she certainly wasn't hot. Every time I stopped bouncing her she would stop making the sound, only to start again as soon as the bouncing resumed. Chandi was laughing! Bouncing, it would seem, is very funny! Later that day, I found a website that seemed to describe what I had heard, confirming that dogs do indeed laugh.

Chandi very often lies with her body in position first thing in the morning, waiting for me to bounce her up and down. Each time I do, she grins and, yes, she laughs too.

Our hat-trick of wins, including the Crufts competition, was a fabulous start to 2005. Having worked so hard, I felt we all deserved a break, so I spent some time taking Pepper and Chandi out for long walks to all our favourite places, and on day trips to Lake Vyrnwy and the beach, which we thoroughly enjoyed.

After a few months of just enjoying being together and

exploring new places, I received an email out of the blue from a researcher at ITV, asking if Chandi and I would like to audition for a new television talent show. They had found my website as they were searching for potential acts to invite to the auditions and they had liked the sound of us. It turned out that they were making a pilot programme, and if that was liked by the executives at ITV, a series would follow.

I was excited at the prospect of being involved in another television show with Chandi and this sounded like the show of my dreams! I checked that the audition room would have a carpeted surface so there was no possibility of Chandi slipping and potentially injuring herself. They also promised not to keep Chandi waiting in a large queue for hours before we auditioned; we were to go straight in when we arrived. This was everything I needed to hear and I confirmed that we wanted to audition.

Our audition would be held in Manchester one Sunday in August, so we had a few weeks to prepare a short routine. The audition happened to take place the day after an event we were going to in Windsor called the Wag and Bone Show. We were entering a class called Pup Idol, in which each entrant would have two minutes to showcase their dog's talents.

That weekend was very busy. It was a good eight-hour

round trip to Windsor, after a very early start. Then, after spending all day at the show, we had to get up very early on the Sunday to make it up to Manchester in time for the audition. We were so tired that morning and I wasn't feeling on top form as I hadn't slept very well, but I knew I'd regret it if we didn't go. I got out of bed, started the day and bundled the dogs into the car.

When we arrived at the venue in Manchester, the queue of people waiting to audition stretched down the street, and it was still an hour before the auditions were due to start. Fortunately I found a well-shaded parking spot down a side road opposite the venue and Chandi and I left Pepper in the car. I felt slightly embarrassed going to the front of the queue, but we walked towards the lad holding a clipboard, who asked our names and then told us to go inside and register.

We were taken up the stairs to the audition room. There were two other people waiting and they looked very nervous. We nodded to each other and then all of us went back to concentrating on our own thoughts in preparation for our auditions. I started to quietly warm up with Chandi and we tried out a couple of tricks.

When it was our turn, a researcher showed us into a large, empty room with a row of windows along one wall and some carpet in the centre of the floor. The dark grey carpet did nothing to soften the austerity of the room and I could suddenly feel my heart pounding in my chest. Taking a breath to steady myself, I introduced ourselves to the producer, who was sat behind a large desk. A cameraman operated a single camera aimed at the carpeted area where we were to perform.

I handed our CD to the producer and explained that he would be able to hear me giving Chandi commands over the music and that this was not the way the routine was supposed to be seen. I was told not to worry and Chandi and I went to the centre of the floor ready to start.

I used the short two-minute routine Chandi and I had prepared for the Pup Idol contest, set to a somewhat obscure piece of film music called 'March', written by the famous film composer John Williams. I was so self-conscious during that routine as I knew the producer could clearly hear every command I gave to Chandi. I was decidedly uncomfortable by the time we had finished, even though it had gone quite well, considering the strange and stressful circumstances.

The producer called us over to the desk and I crouched down next to Chandi, continually stroking her, to answer his questions, but I was asked if I could stand up as they wanted to film my replies and the camera wasn't getting a good view of me. Feeling a little foolish, I had no choice but to leave the comfort of Chandi's side while I talked about how long we'd been working together, our achievements and the fact that she was a rescue dog.

The producer didn't comment on anything I said; he just nodded and made notes on the paper in front of him. When he had run out of questions for me, he thanked me and said we could leave.

Chandi and I walked to the corner of the room and I opened the door, then accidentally dropped Chandi's lead. I bent down to pick it up, and as I was standing up, I heard the producer comment to the cameraman, 'That dog was—'

Before he could finish his sentence, the cameraman said, 'Shhhhhhhhhh!' as he must have realized that I hadn't actually left the room yet.

I quickly did, and wished I hadn't heard the first part of the sentence without knowing how it ended. Was the last word 'rubbish' or 'incredible'? The researcher waiting outside the audition room thanked me and informed me that if we had been successful, we would get either a call or a letter within a couple of weeks, but that they weren't acknowledging unsuccessful acts. As soon as I had thanked the researcher, Chandi and I left the building as quickly as we could and went to find Pepper, who was lying on her back along the rear seat of the car, fast asleep.

After a week had slowly gone by, and I had convinced

myself that I would never hear anything about it as we must have been unsuccessful, to my utter surprise I received a phone message asking me to call one of the producers and giving the number to ring.

I called straight away and the voice that answered was very warm and friendly when I said my name. She swiftly told me that they had all loved watching the tape of our audition and that Chandi was amazing. She went on to say that they would love to have us in the pilot of the new talent show! We talked further and I was really excited. The producer explained how the show was going to work, with all the contestants sat among the audience. Each contestant would be called down from the audience when it was their turn to perform.

When I heard their plans, though, my heart sank. There was no way I could ask Chandi to sit among an audience in a hot studio and then get up and perform. I needed to warm her up so she wouldn't be in danger of straining a muscle or injuring herself in any way, and I needed her to be focused on me. I was firmly told that there were to be no exceptions, so I had no choice other than to politely thank the producer for selecting us in the first place and decline the invitation.

The pilot show was called *Paul O'Grady's Got Talent*, which was to become none other than *Britain's Got Talent* when it debuted in the UK eighteen months later.

I was bitterly disappointed at missing this chance, but I didn't regret my decision in the slightest. Chandi is the most important thing in my life and I always do my best to put her needs head and shoulders above any desires I may have, no matter how much I longed for the excitement of more television opportunities. I told myself that if we were indeed to be on television again one day, then an opportunity that didn't involve me compromising Chandi in any way would present itself when the time was right. In fact I was strangely convinced of it.

EIGHT

It's Happening Again

So far 2005 had been an eventful and rewarding year, but there was to be a sting in the tail. It was November, just three months after our talent show audition. About a week after Pepper had been in season, she suddenly started drinking copious amounts of water. I watched her closely for a day and then made an emergency appointment with our vet.

I knew that excessive thirst is a sign of a nasty and life-threatening uterine infection called pyometra, which can happen after a bitch has been in season. I rang the vet and explained, and was told to bring Pepper over. Blood tests were taken to check for signs of infection, and I took Pepper home to wait for the results. When the results came back, her white blood cell count was extremely elevated, and even though Pepper had not shown any signs of discomfort when the vet had palpated her abdomen, and wasn't off her food, the vet confirmed that my poor Pepper did indeed have pyometra. She needed emergency surgery to remove her ovaries and uterus, which were very infected.

Just as I had been when Pepper had got the bone stuck in her throat, I was terrified that I was going to lose my precious dog under general anaesthetic. There was also the risk that something would rupture inside her and the infection would spread. I knew there was no alternative, though, so I gently hugged her and told her how much I loved her before the vet gave her the anaesthetic and she went limp in my arms.

Chandi and I sat in the car waiting for the operation to be over. I hoped and prayed that everything was going well. After about an hour and a half, the door I was watching opened and the vet came out to see me. Pepper had made it through the surgery and everything had been removed without any ruptures. The infection had been very bad, however, and though the source of the pyometra had been completely removed, the tremendous response Pepper's immune system had mounted against the infection would take its toll on her and she was going to need time to recover. She was put on antibiotics to prevent any further infection due to the surgery.

I went in to be with Pepper as she came round from the anaesthetic. She looked so small and vulnerable lying on the blanket with a tube hanging out of the side of her mouth. I put my face near hers and spoke gently to her, telling her that everything was going to be all right, at the same time trying to make myself believe it.

By now it was after surgery hours and apart from me, Pepper and the vet, the veterinary hospital was empty. Chandi and I stayed with Pepper all night, Chandi lying in her bed and only getting out once to say hello to the vet when she came in to check on Pepper. After examining Pepper, she left us alone for a couple of hours. I lay on the floor next to Pepper and the only way I knew she was alive was by watching her chest rise and fall. She just stared blankly ahead and wouldn't move.

The vet came to check on Pepper every two hours throughout the night as her heart was quite weak after the surgery. I've had some horrible and terrifying nights in my life, but this was among the worst I'd known. There was nothing I could do for her other than stay with her and let her know I loved her.

Her paws were terribly cold, so I put the fleecy blankets I'd brought with us over her and rubbed her paws to help them warm up. She was holding her own but just wouldn't get up, despite the vet's encouragement. Pepper wouldn't move for me, either. I could tell the vet was worried, but she told me just to let her rest and she'd be back in an hour or so.

I didn't sleep at all that night; I was too desperately

worried about Pepper. But then, without warning, at 6.20 a.m., Pepper suddenly got to her feet and, before I could get up, walked stiffly over to the door. Pepper turned to look at me and then looked at the door again.

'It's OK, I'm coming,' I told her as I staggered to my feet. I was so pleased to see Pepper up. I went to the door and opened it. She walked slowly to the grass and had the most enormous wee imaginable. She had had fluids run into her during and after the surgery, and this was the first time she had emptied herself since before the operation, over fourteen hours earlier.

Once she felt better, she looked up at me and then started to walk over to our car. I gently held on to her, as she was unsteady on her feet, but she insisted on walking to the car. She stood by the door asking to get in. There was nothing more I wanted to do than take her home, but I told her that she would have to wait for the vet to give the all clear and I guided a reluctant Pepper back into the hospital. A few minutes later, the vet came to check on her and deemed her well enough to go home.

It took Pepper a few days to recover, and the first couple of nights at home were awful. Pepper just couldn't seem to lie down and she didn't know what she wanted. She would pace up and down until she was so tired she had to go to sleep, but even then she was extremely restless. I slept on the sofa as Pepper was unable to climb the stairs after her surgery and I needed to stay nearby.

I was so relieved when she started to feel better and she could go for short walks again. She recovered quickly, considering how poorly she had been, and was soon back to her old self. All the while Pepper had been poorly, Chandi had been so good and was quite happy for the majority of my attention to go to Pepper, knowing she needed it more.

I took both dogs to Pets at Home to choose what they wanted for Christmas. We looked through all the toys together and I bought every single one that they showed interest in, to put in their stockings for Christmas Day. Even though we were spending Christmas on our own, as was usual now, I couldn't help thinking how lucky we were to all be together. Things could have turned out very differently.

One day in February 2006, I received a phone call from a researcher called Katie, who was working on the BBC's *Blue Peter*. She said that the programme was doing a live competition, and were looking for five dogs with different skills.

They had read about Chandi on our website and wanted to invite her to be the 'dancing dog' on the show. I was so excited and over the next couple of weeks we sorted out the finer details and I decided to cut down a new routine we'd been working on, performed to 'Don't Rain on My Parade', to the ninety seconds that they wanted. They also offered us our own dressing room so I could safely leave Pepper while Chandi and I were in the studio.

When the show finished on BBC One, it would continue for a few more minutes on the satellite channel CBBC, and the winner of the Pup Idol contest, voted for by the viewers, would then be given a couple of minutes to show more of what they could do. Just in case we won the contest, Chandi and I rehearsed two versions of the routine.

The show was to be broadcast on 16 March 2006, and we were very excited, but quite nervous as we had only done live TV once before, when we did the short performance on *Children in Need* back in 2001. Even though our performances at shows were always live, being on television added more pressure.

Our 'Don't Rain on My Parade' routine involved several props. We worked with a hat and an umbrella, and I also wanted to use a wooden chair so Chandi could interact with it to create some new moves. At one point, I would stand on the chair acting like I was losing my balance, holding the open umbrella like an old-style tightrope walker. Meanwhile, Chandi sat next to the chair, resting her front paws on the seat and dipping her nose down between her front feet to hide her eyes, as though unable to watch me wobbling about on the chair. The move was quite effective and fitted beautifully with the lyrics, and Chandi would get into position unassisted on just a verbal cue.

Chandi and I came up with many other moves with the chair, but whenever she ran forward and jumped up to put her front paws on it, she would invariably knock it over. If it didn't fall down, it would do a huge, scary wobble, which unsettled her. I needed the chair to be rock steady and didn't quite know what to do, so I phoned Roy and asked if he would be able to figure out how to weight the chair without spoiling its appearance. Roy was always on hand if I needed help with anything, and I was so grateful, as I didn't have anyone else to call on.

The first weight he tried was really heavy, and we were both hopeful that it would do the job, but when Chandi tried it out, there was still a worrying wobble. The problem was that whatever he used to weight the chair had to sit underneath the seat and be small enough that it didn't ruin the aesthetics of the chair and distract the audience. A few days later, Roy rang to say he had a solution.

We drove over the next day with some trepidation, as

Roy had told me if this didn't work, then he wasn't sure what else to do. I sent Chandi running to the chair and she jumped up and hit it with her front paws. The chair didn't move an inch!

'That's fabulous!' I exclaimed, and Chandi tried it another couple of times from different angles and at varying speeds. Each time Chandi hit the chair, it stayed motionless and I could see her confidence grow each time she tried it out. I asked what he'd put on it, as the modification was not obvious.

'I've taken the wheel weight off my rotavator and bolted it to the underneath of the seat,' Roy replied.

I went over to have a look and tried tipping the chair. I wasn't expecting it to be so heavy, and to anyone who didn't know the chair had been modified, I would have looked rather feeble. The effort it took to tip it to look underneath was considerably more than my brain was telling me was necessary.

The new iron addition to the chair weighed forty pounds, and in order for the originally rather flimsy chair to be able to hold that much weight without collapsing, Roy had had to add some metal supports to the legs and seat. He had also painted the whole thing black for me, as I had mentioned what I was going to do, and fixed some nonslip rubbery material that I had bought to the wooden seat to make it safer when

Chandi or I had to put our feet on the chair. Roy had done a marvellous job.

Lifting this really heavy chair in and out of the car every day in order to practise was a bit of a nightmare, but the effort was worth it. To thank Roy for his efforts, I invited him along to *Blue Peter* with us and he was excited about visiting the iconic doughnut-shaped BBC building that is Television Centre, as were we.

Finally 16 March arrived, and despite the heavy snowfall that we had experienced in the days before, we had been able to rehearse sufficiently. Television Centre was just as I remembered it from my visits as a child. In fact the only thing that had changed was that the statue of Petra, one of the *Blue Peter* dogs, was no longer in front of the building but had been moved to the *Blue Peter* garden.

We had been told to wait in reception for Katie, the researcher I had been speaking to over the weeks, to come down and escort us to the studio. Reception was quite busy with people coming and going, so no one really paid any attention to Pepper or Chandi, other than to glance in their direction occasionally. Lots of people were walking past us, including Rob Brydon, who wandered through on his way to the lifts. Pepper was starting to get a little bored, so I thought I'd liven things up a little. I nudged Roy and he instantly grinned, shook his head and covered his ears. He knew what I was about to do.

'Pepper,' I said in a soft voice, 'do you want to say, "Woof"?'

Obviously Pepper quite fancied the idea as she obligingly let out the biggest bark she could manage.

'Wooooooooooffff!'

The acoustics of the building really helped to carry the noise, and even I was startled at the sheer volume, with subtle reverberation, Pepper had been able to create. We felt the air in reception move as everyone jumped and temporarily stopped speaking. A second later and everything carried on as normal. No one knew that I had instigated the bark. Pepper was all too happy to take the blame and looked decidedly pleased with her contribution.

I had taught Pepper to bark on command when I had had the idea of getting her to bark in the correct places in the song 'How Much Is That Doggy in the Window?' I would play it on the piano with Pepper sitting close by. After a few attempts, we perfected our rendition and would make visitors to the house laugh when we gave an impromptu performance. Pepper would sit by the piano stool looking up at the music, and I had taught her that when she heard me sharply draw in my breath, she would bark. I could get her to bark either once or twice depending on how many times I cued her with my breath, and she was always exactly in time. No one ever realized how we did it, as it looked as though Pepper was reading the music. In fact very often in her later years, when we did it, she would bark in the correct places without me having to cue her at all. She had to have been listening to the music.

Katie arrived and we were taken down to our dressing room. Then, after making sure Pepper was comfortable in her bed, Katie, Roy, Chandi and I went down to the studio for the first rehearsal. Waiting outside in the quiet of the tea bar, *Blue Peter* presenter Gethin Jones walked past – in a sarong, I might add – and waved to us. We went into the studio and our eyes adjusted to the bright lights and all the activity. The other presenters on the show were messing around and laughing at jokes and everything seemed very relaxed, until we were introduced to a rather irritated-sounding floor manager, who started to tell me, along with the other handlers and their dogs, how things were going to work.

As I was first in the line-up, I really needed to pay attention to the directions because there would be no one in front of me to follow. Each of the dogs was to stand on a little podium that had their name written on the front, and one by one we were to walk forward onto the green carpet and, when the music started, do whatever it was we were there to do. Chandi and I needed our chair to be brought in for our routine and I was amused to see all the crew have a go at lifting the chair and examining it to see why it was so heavy. When they'd worked it out, it was put in position.

I began feeling a bit hot under the collar right about then, as there was no way I was going to wear my glasses and I wouldn't really be able to see the floor manager's cue to start moving without them. In the end, by squinting ever so slightly, I just about managed to see the wildly waving arms of the floor manager and moved at the correct time.

Chandi and I ran through our ninety-second routine without a hitch and were asked to do it once more for the director to get the best shots of us from the cameras. We then went back to our dressing room to relax. After a quick romp round the *Blue Peter* garden with both dogs, we were back in the studio for one final rehearsal and then it was time for the live show.

I felt incredibly sick and nervous the second I heard our names called and we had to walk out to perform our routine. All I could think was that this was live television. Things could have gone badly wrong for us then, as I really was scared. I had two choices: mess things up for Chandi through nerves, or get a grip. I chose the latter option and my nerves died down when

I thought: Well, it may be live, with millions watching, but I can't see them, so let's just pretend that they're not out there!

Despite my initial nerves, Chandi gave an absolutely fabulous performance, packed with many of our best moves, including the back-to-back and holding the umbrella with both front paws. She was fast and really accurate with every move, and clearly enjoyed herself. Once we had taken a bow together, we moved back and Chandi jumped up on her little podium. Then we watched the other four dogs take their turn in front of the cameras.

The second dog played basketball with a tiny child's basketball hoop – dropping the ball through the hoop. The third jumped over a skipping rope with her owner, and the fourth dog gave a fun performance on a skate-board. The final dog did some impressive 'keepy-uppy' by bouncing the football on his nose.

Later in the show, the viewers voted and the winner was announced. It was Chandi! This meant that after walking over to the presenters to be given our trophy, we had to perform the longer version of our routine. We had just a few seconds to get into position, and as I was hurrying onto the carpet, looking down at Chandi, the man rushing in with the chair crashed straight into me and cracked his head against mine. I reeled backwards, putting my hand up to my head, and heard the entire studio laugh.

I had precisely two seconds to compose myself before the music for the routine started and we had to perform. Fortunately it was only me who had been injured; Chandi was unhurt, as was the props man. In fact Chandi seemed completely unfazed by the considerable silent activity in the studio. She was comfortable with the lights, the heat, the fast-moving cameras and all the people – she was completely professional and performed amazingly.

As we were leaving the studio, I was asked if I wanted to take the trophy we had won home with us. I looked at it and then shot a sideways glance at Roy, who was stood next to me. The trophy was a huge bone-shaped piece of polystyrene fixed on a short pole to a wooden plinth and spray-painted gold.

I paused to consider my decision and then said, 'Hmm, tempting, but no, thank you.'

The man holding it replied, 'Funny, I thought you'd say that,' and laughed as he walked away, taking the monstrous trophy with him.

We came away from Television Centre tired but happy and with a very successful live television perfor-mance securely under our belts, plus a treasured *Blue Peter* badge in my pocket. The six-hour round trip to London, along with the stress of the performances, had left me exhausted and I was glad when we finally got home. I couldn't wait to feed the dogs and go to bed. Before I went to sleep, though, I watched our performance, which I'd recorded on my Sky+ box. Chandi looked even better than I had thought she did! Every move was perfect and she looked so keen and happy to be performing. With each performance we gave, we were improving, and it was clear to anyone watching that Chandi was having so much fun.

Now that Crufts held an official competition for Heelwork to Music and Freestyle, there were qualifying competitions throughout the year. I had decided to enter Chandi in a qualifying competition for the following year's Crufts at All About Dogs, which was being held as usual in May. I had also decided just to go down for the day, after the unpleasant tent and caravan experiences of previous years. It was a long way to drive in a day, but if we did this competition and Chandi qualified, we wouldn't have to do any more shows that year. Instead we could spend our time having trips to the beach and relaxing on long walks, enjoying being together.

All About Dogs was a great show with lots going on besides the Heelwork to Music and Freestyle shows, and this year – 2006 – there was no mud to contend with and the weather was fine and dry! Once we had arrived on the showground and had handed our music to the show steward, Pepper, Chandi and I went for a wander to see what else there was to do. After looking at the various rings, we found a pay-as-you-go agility ring with a complete range of equipment set up in a rather inviting course.

Pepper noticed the equipment and I saw her ears go up. It had been years since we had done a proper full-blown agility course. The last agility show we had been to was back in 1998, and although we had set up equipment in our garden and played around with that, I could see that Pepper wanted to have a go in the ring.

The ring was securely fenced all the way round and there was no way for Pepper to get out, so I paid the one-pound entry fee and we all walked in. I would have loved to have had a go with Chandi as well, but I didn't dare before the Heelwork to Music and Freestyle classes we had entered, just in case she hurt herself and we had to withdraw. Chandi obligingly settled down to watch Pepper, and after walking the course to study the order of the obstacles, Pepper and I went to the start. She was keen to get going, but she waited until I had run just past the first jump and yelled, 'Go!' before diving in.

She shot over the first jump, then the second, and the third, with me already trailing behind, despite running as fast as I could. I caught up with her at the A-frame as she ran up the steep front ramp and then slowed to negotiate the apex and hurtled down the other side. I told her to slow down and she did, touching the contact area perfectly.

Next came the weave poles and I directed her into them and encouraged her through as her little furry body swiftly snaked from side to side. Then she was on to more jumps, clearing each perfectly, and then through the tunnel and over more jumps to the seesaw. She remembered to wait in the middle for the other side of the seesaw to hit the ground and then raced off and through the next tunnel chute. Two more jumps and we had finished!

It was so much fun and Pepper was jumping around me very excitedly. I caught hold of her and kissed her on her head and then turned as the lady in charge of the ring came over to talk to us. As the ring was completely enclosed, I didn't worry about Pepper and thought she would wander over to Chandi, who hadn't moved from where she had originally settled down to watch.

'Do you compete with her?' the lady asked.

'No,' I replied, 'but we tried it a long time ago.'

'She was brilliant!' said the lady, and then asked, 'How old is she?'

'Almost thirteen,' I said.

The lady couldn't believe Pepper was that old and

asked what I fed her. I told her all about the completely organic bones and raw-food diet with plenty of freshly juiced organic fruit and vegetables, and she was amazed. I had continued feeding bones even after Pepper had had the accident with the chicken bone getting lodged in her throat a few years previously. I didn't feed them whole any more, though; I would sit for ages cutting up chicken carcasses into tiny pieces so it would never happen again.

Suddenly the lady asked with a giggle, 'What is she doing in your bag?'

I turned quickly to see that Pepper had her head stuck inside a bag and was definitely doing something she shouldn't.

'It's not my bag,' I replied as I went over to stop Pepper doing whatever it was she was doing.

'Oh, right. It must belong to the lady who is supposed to be running this ring. I'm only here while she went to get a cup of coffee.'

As she said that, I managed to pull Pepper's head out of the bag, and as I did so, much to my combined horror and amusement, we both could clearly see exactly what Pepper had been doing. Dangling limply from her teeth was what looked like a cheese and pickle sandwich.

I told Pepper to drop it and she obligingly spat it out. I caught it and closed my eyes briefly as I realized that it was covered in slobber and had a very definite pattern of teeth marks in the bread. I looked up at the lady stood next to me, there was a brief silence, and then we both burst out laughing.

The woman soon scurried away to get her own bag and waved as she shot out of the ring. I felt bad as I knew what I was going to do next. I shoved the soggy sandwich back in the bag, yelled for the dogs to come to me and made a speedy exit.

Later that same day, Chandi and I qualified for both the Heelwork to Music and the Freestyle Crufts final competitions. From 2006 the two disciplines would now have separate final competitions at Crufts held on consecutive days, instead of the previous combined event. The following year the qualifying system would change again, introducing semi-finals to the process. We drove home exhausted but happy, with me still giggling about the sandwich incident.

Summer soon arrived and the dogs and I enjoyed some beautiful walks in the hills. One afternoon, though, Pepper wouldn't get out of the car. This was very unusual, as she was normally keen to be running about as soon as possible. I gently lifted her down and she just stood where I put her. I felt her all over to see if I could find anything wrong, but there was nothing obvious, so I asked her again if she wanted to go and this time she wandered off. I locked the car and Chandi and I followed behind. We didn't go far that afternoon: if there was something wrong with Pepper, I didn't want to make it worse by letting her have too much exercise.

The next morning, we arrived at that day's walk destination and I opened the car door for Pepper. Again she didn't want to get out. This continued for several days before I phoned the vet. Pepper was eating and drinking fine, and seemed happy in herself; the only symptom was that she just did not want to go for a walk. It was peculiar, because Pepper loved going out and exploring, and I was concerned.

After examining Pepper, the vet announced that she couldn't find anything obviously wrong with her either, but maybe she had hurt a tendon or ligament in her leg and it was hurting when she exercised. That was the only explanation the vet could come up with and I was told to rest her for ten days to see if the situation improved, which it didn't.

I took Pepper back to the vet, but she was at a loss as to what was wrong with Pepper and the situation went on for weeks, with me becoming increasingly concerned about her. I decided to mix up some slippery elm powder to give to Pepper four times a day. Whenever either of the dogs had an upset tummy, I would give them this herbal powder, as it has a very powerful soothing and healing action. Unbelievably, after one day, Pepper wanted to go for a walk for the first time in weeks. The slippery elm was helping whatever it was that was causing her problem. This was good news and I continued with the powder for a few months. When Pepper had no further problems and was back to her usual self, I stopped giving it to her and didn't give it another thought.

One night in December 2006, though, Pepper woke me up telling me she was going to be sick. Her back was hunched up, and when she finally vomited, I was horrified to see that there was blood in it. My heart sank and before I could clean the first lot up, she brought up more and this time there was more blood. Even though it was about 3 a.m., I had no choice but to ring the vet, who told me to take Pepper to the surgery.

I dressed and got both dogs into the car for the thirty-mile trip to our holistic vet. Pepper had settled a little and wasn't sick again in the car. When we got to the surgery, the vet greeted us and Pepper was X-rayed. Nothing was unusual on the X-ray, but the vet thought she may have a stomach ulcer and sent us home with some medication to reduce the stomach acid and give it a chance to heal. I had an uneasy feeling about the diagnosis and didn't give Pepper the pills, but instead put her back on the slippery elm multiple times a day.

Again we had no further problems, and whether it

was an ulcer or just a warning of what was to come a few months later, I don't know, but for the time being, everything was back to normal. The uneasy feeling I had stayed with me, though, and our time together suddenly became even more precious.

NINE

The Hardest Goodbye

At the beginning of December, I received two emails within a couple of days of each other, both completely out of the blue. I was stunned to see one waiting for me in my inbox when I logged on while the dogs had a snooze after their morning walk. It was from a researcher, inviting Chandi and me back to audition for the first series of what was now called *Britain's Got Talent*, after we had turned down the pilot show eighteen months previously. The show had been aired in America and was now being made into a series in the UK. The second email came from the BBC, inviting us to audition for another talent show called *When Will I Be Famous?*

After a few emails back and forth to the two researchers, I had a decision to make. I had to choose between the shows; there was no way I would be allowed to appear on both with them being aired so close together. I was delighted at the prospect of being involved in a huge show with Chandi. I chose to go for *When Will I Be Famous?* and was told to go to an audition in Birmingham on 8 January 2007 at the Hippodrome Theatre. I was excited about doing some more TV with Chandi since our performance on *Blue Peter* had gone so well.

I was moving house on 4 January and spent Christmas frantically packing, in between preparing an audition piece for Chandi. I had moved five times in ten years and was dreading moving day and then the first night in a new house, alone, feeling very unsettled. Pepper and Chandi were not worried in any way by all the boxes piling up around them. As long as they were with me and we were together, they knew everything was just fine. It made me feel better too.

The new house was slightly bigger than where we currently lived and it had a small, separate dining room that I could use as a music room. I knew I was doing the right thing moving, as instead of travelling miles to all my various piano and violin pupils' houses, I could once again teach from my own home. It also meant I would not have to spend so much time away from Pepper and Chandi, which I truly hated.

Moving day came and it was long and exhausting. When all the many boxes were finally deposited in my new home and the removal men had left, the house was very quiet and it was just me and the dogs stood looking at one another. The first and most important thing to do was sort their beds out and unpack all their toys so they felt more at home. After doing that and preparing their food, I set about unpacking the boxes that were surrounding me. In other circumstances I might have taken my time, but I knew that if by any chance Chandi and I were successful at the audition in just four days' time, a film crew would be sent to the house to interview us. A house full of boxes wouldn't make the best impression.

We all set off for Birmingham very early the day of the audition to make our 10 a.m. slot. With both dogs by my side, as well as a collapsible dog crate for Pepper to sit in while I auditioned with Chandi, we made our way from the car park to the Hippodrome and were met by a researcher.

We were taken straight up to one of the audition rooms, and I started to warm Chandi up in our usual way in the area outside the door. When it was our turn to go in, Pepper had to come too. As I didn't want to run the risk of her interrupting Chandi and me while we were mid-routine, I had to spend a few minutes putting up the crate and settling her inside. She was very good and as soon as I opened the door to the crate, she went inside and lay down. There were about ten people in the room, along with several cameramen. The room was set out like a small theatre with a stage area and a few rows of tiered seating, and I was aware that I was holding up proceedings, as they had a lot of other people queueing up outside.

I felt nervous and was glad when the music started and Chandi and I could just concentrate on performing.

For our ninety-second audition I choreographed a routine that showcased Chandi's cleverest moves to the fast-moving, catchy tune of Perez Prado's 'Guaglione'. When we struck our final pose, there was a smattering of applause from the people watching us. One person then stepped forward to introduce herself.

'Hi, I'm Helen,' she said as she grasped my hand and shook it. 'That was an absolutely amazing performance. Were you pleased with it?'

'It's always nerve-racking performing in a small room where everyone can hear me giving Chandi the cues for the moves,' I replied.

'Oh, don't worry about that. I was so mesmerized just watching you two, I didn't even give it any thought!'

I was feeling a little relieved by now, as I didn't think the performance had been anywhere near as good as it could have been. I was pleased that our audition had got such a warm reception.

'You may well be hearing from us soon,' Helen went on to say, 'but for now,' she said, anxiously glancing at her watch, 'we have to get on, as we have so many other people to see.'

'Of course. I understand. Thank you so much for everything,' I said as I hurried over to Pepper, unzipped the collapsible crate, allowing Pepper her freedom, and then dragged everything as quickly as I could through the door, which someone kindly held open for me.

We were briefly interviewed outside the audition room, and the cameraman said hello and that he remembered us from *Blue Peter* the previous year! Once the interview was over, we were told that if we had been successful, we would receive a telephone call very soon.

The following day, Chandi, Pepper and I had just got back to the house after our walk when I saw I had a message from Helen, the producer we had met at the audition the day before. I hadn't been expecting a call, despite her enthusiastic reception at the audition, and I certainly hadn't been expecting one this soon. She had left a number for me to ring and asked me to phone her as soon as possible. I dialled immediately.

'It's Tina. She's on the phone now!' she said to someone, after greeting me. Then to me, 'If you and Chandi still want to, we would love to have you on the show.'

I was ecstatic, but couldn't think of anything to say and could only grin at the dogs. Luckily she spoke first.

'As soon as we met you and Chandi and saw you perform, it was an absolute no-brainer that we would want you on the show! We loved your relationship with Chandi and it really shone through when you performed. Chandi is amazingly clever and we've never seen a dog do those kinds of things before!'

I was really touched by her kind words. It suddenly dawned on me that this was the biggest television programme we had been involved in and I felt very excited!

Helen said that the first show was to take place on 20 January, with the pilot being made the week before. They wanted Chandi and me to do the pilot as well, which I thought was a great idea, as it would give us a chance to practise in the studio before the first proper live show.

A researcher called later that day to sort out the details and the next couple of weeks turned into a whirlwind. I never seemed to be off the phone to the BBC and I barely had a minute to breathe. It was all so exciting, but I was under strict instructions to keep my good news entirely to myself. I did ring Roy, though – I just had to tell someone! I was really looking forward to going back to Television Centre with Chandi and Pepper. We travelled down to London the Thursday before the pilot show, which was being filmed on the Saturday. Once we arrived at the hotel, a car arrived to take us all to the studio for a meeting with the producers and the first rehearsal.

After settling Pepper in our dressing room, Chandi and I went into the studio, which turned out to be the same one that I had played the piano in for the last ever *Jim'll Fix It*, which was a celebration and look back at twenty years of the show. I had been the only 'Fix-ee' invited to perform, probably because of my long association with the programme and the fact that I was the only person to have been awarded two *Jim'll Fix It* badges! On that occasion, I was a soloist playing with a live band, and without my childhood hero Jonathan Cohen.

The studio was now painted very black for *When Will I Be Famous?* and looked impressive. Chandi and I sat in the audience and watched someone else rehearsing on the stage until it was our turn. When we were called up, Chandi seemed calm and focused, and after limbering up, they played our music and we did our first run-through.

It didn't go terribly well. This studio was very different to anywhere we had performed before and the black set felt oppressive, though I could see that it would look fabulous on screen. I watched Chandi carefully and sensed she wasn't completely happy on the stage. She had been fine during the warm-up, but the stage was different. She improved after a second run-through with more encouragement and we were given plenty of time to play on the stage and become familiar with it. More rehearsals followed the next day, with a full dress rehearsal on Saturday before the evening pilot show in front of a studio audience and three judges. I grew more confident as I saw Chandi relax and I think we both managed to enjoy the performance for the pilot show.

After the pilot, we drove home, and before returning to London the following Thursday for the first of the live shows, a film crew came over for the day to get some footage of us at home and do a short interview. This would be aired before our performance.

I was told to prepare for a very long day. The crew arrived in the morning and aimed to set up in the living room to film me talking about Chandi and how we were feeling about being on the show. We were then to head up to the Long Mynd to be filmed working against the beautiful backdrop.

On the day of filming, with the camera and the huge lights set up in my living room, there was barely room to move and Pepper was making an incredible racket upstairs. As she wasn't taking part in the filming, I'd thought it would be better to keep her out of the way, but she wanted to see what was going on at all times and told us so. In the end, I had to let her come downstairs to keep her quiet.

It was a good job the crew were dog lovers – there wasn't any room to move and the only vantage point Pepper could find where she wasn't in the way was if she stood with her head jammed between the cameraman's knees. Nobody minded and she happily stood there for as long as we were filming with a grin on her face. She was as good as gold.

When Thursday came, we drove back to London for more rehearsals and then the actual show. This time I sat in the make-up area for a couple of hours while the team expertly did my hair and make-up, and the costume designer even put together a smart black outfit for me with a white waistcoat.

Seeing the audience filing into the studio made everything seem very real. All the acts were on stage for the introduction to the show, hosted by Graham Norton. Chandi and I were to perform towards the end, and while we were waiting I played with Chandi, getting her keen and excited, ready for our routine.

When it was time for us to get into position on the stage, I felt nervous, but I looked down at Chandi and she seemed unperturbed. The audience made a lot of noise as we walked out, but Chandi just kept walking, looking up at me and concentrating like a true professional. I relaxed a little, the music started and I worked hard to encourage Chandi to sparkle and put maximum effort into every movement.

I was relieved when the music ended and we held our final back-to-back position for a few seconds as the applause started and we took a bow. Graham Norton then met us on the stage to listen to the judges' verdicts – two of them loved us, but one American guy wasn't so keen, as he was more used to the type of acts he could book to perform in nightclubs!

The show's format pitched one act directly against another – Chandi and I went up against a young male singer – and only one of these acts went through to the next round, when the audience at home would vote for their favourites. The top two acts would go head to head in the final.

Later on, I was delighted when it was announced that Chandi and I were one of the two acts through to the final. We had to perform again and our second time went a little better than the first – I was certainly more relaxed, and we just went for it with all the energy we could muster, as we had nothing to lose.

After Chandi and I and the other competing act had performed, we stood at opposite ends of the stage. Graham Norton was in the centre building up the anticipation and tension in the studio as he prepared to reveal the winner.

'The name of the winning act is . . .' Huge pause while tense music played. '. . . Tina and Chandi!'

The audience went wild. I couldn't believe that we had won and bent down to stroke Chandi, who was wagging her tail furiously, so much so that her whole body was swinging from side to side. Graham Norton came over to talk to us and told us that we had just won £10,000! He then asked if we would come back the following week to defend our title. I hadn't realized that the winner of the show had to come back the following week and compete again, but I was happy that our exciting time wasn't yet over.

We drove home the following day, still reeling from the excitement and winning the prize money. We had a phone call the following day from the BBC press office, who had received a request from *Richard and Judy* for Chandi and me to be guests on the Channel Four show that week. I was delighted – Mum had always watched *Richard and Judy* – and I wished even more that Mum and Dad were still here to see everything that was happening. I couldn't quite believe that we would be sitting on the sofa with Richard and Judy!

We drove to London early on Tuesday and were met by a BBC camera crew, who were going to follow us for the day at the *Richard and Judy* studio in order to make the clip introducing our next performance the following week on *When Will I Be Famous?* It was the coolest thing having our own camera crew with us and we thoroughly enjoyed ourselves! The *Richard and Judy* researcher led us to the dressing room they'd arranged so I could leave Pepper to wait for Chandi and me in a safe place. Guests usually wait in the green room, but I couldn't leave Pepper in a public place unattended, so they had kindly given us the only spare dressing room.

Quite used to arriving at unusual places, both Pepper and Chandi took everything in their stride, stopping politely to say hello to everyone we met as we were shown to our dressing room, one of only three in the studio. The other two were occupied by Richard and Judy. It was the nicest dressing room we've ever been in, with fresh flowers, a bowl of fruit and, on the table, a beautifully wrapped gift with my name on it. I opened it to find a box of expensive toiletries and a nice card from the show's producer. We made ourselves at home and Richard Madeley popped in before we went on air to say hello. He was very friendly and charming, and greeted both Pepper and Chandi warmly.

Our interview went well – I had no idea of the questions I was going to be asked in advance, but I think I came out with some relatively intelligent and coherent answers, and Chandi looked gorgeous sat on the sofa. We ended the show with a performance of our winning routine and Chandi did it fabulously, as usual.

It took a few days to adjust to what had happened and

believe that it was actually real. I had agreed to come back to *When Will I Be Famous?* the following week and quickly put together a new routine in the six days we had. Sadly we were knocked out in the second show and didn't make the final two that week, but I didn't feel bad at all. We had had the time of our lives and I was just glad we'd made it that far.

When all the excitement was over, it was quite hard to adjust to normal life again and I did feel rather sad. With Crufts only four weeks away, thankfully I had enough to keep me busy. We had qualified at All About Dogs the previous year, but I hadn't prepared a routine yet. Having previously managed to pull together two routines in just three weeks, I could surely manage just one for the Free-style class that year.

I chose 'Mack and Mabel' as our music – I had loved the ice-skating routine that Torvill and Dean had done to the same music a few years before, and their work really inspired my choreography with Chandi. The routine we put together was one of the hardest we had ever done. I packed it with moves and every one really interpreted the varied sections of the music.

The routine was extremely well received at Crufts and we were awarded second place. I have never experienced such a reaction from the audience, and after the results had been announced and I was trying to make my way out of the arena with Chandi, I couldn't move for people I had never met before surrounding us, wanting to congratulate us and tell us how much they had enjoyed our routine. I was very grateful to everyone who took the time to talk to us that day and was delighted that so many people appreciated our routine.

After the excitement of the early part of the year, things settled down again and Pepper, Chandi and I were enjoying going out for long walks in the sunshine. Then completely out of the blue one Thursday afternoon in June, Pepper refused to get out of the car to go for a walk, just as she had done a few months before. I took her over to the vet that same day, but after being thoroughly examined, nothing was found and her blood tests were all apparently normal. The next day she seemed fine, and the following two days she was back to her usual self. However, on the next day, after my last piano pupil left the house on the evening of 26 June, which would have been Mum's birthday, Pepper was obviously in a lot of pain and something was very seriously wrong.

I rang the vet again and we were told to go straight over. I was so worried about my beautiful girl. She was X-rayed and the vet could see something she didn't like the look of in her spleen. I was given three choices: do nothing; open Pepper up and take a look inside; or go to a specialist for an ultrasound scan of her spleen before making a decision.

I decided to take Pepper for the ultrasound scan and made an appointment for the next day at a different vet surgery. To say I was devastated was an understatement, and the uneasy feeling that had persisted in me for all those months was now even more impossible to shake.

During the appointment, Chandi lay on the floor while Pepper had her tummy shaved and a thick gel was applied. I held Pepper on her back, supporting her spine on the hard table while the vet scanned her. He could see a small mass in her spleen and lots of free fluid in her abdomen, which, after a test with a needle, turned out to be blood. My beautiful girl was bleeding internally.

I had to make another decision: we could operate on my almost fourteen-year-old dog to remove her spleen, or do nothing. Pepper was in a lot of pain and there was no time to think it over. I decided to opt for the surgery and telephoned my usual vet to say we were on our way. As soon as we arrived back at her practice, Pepper was to be operated on.

I drove back to the surgery with tears in my eyes but tried to hold it together for Pepper's sake. I didn't want her to sense my emotions and be upset by them. This was major surgery and Pepper wasn't a young dog. She was in a bad way and there was a lot that could go wrong.

Nevertheless, we went ahead, with Chandi and me, as usual, waiting just outside while Pepper was in the operating theatre. There was no way we could go home; I wanted to be as close to her as possible during her ordeal.

After several hours, the vet came out to tell me that Pepper was coming round from the operation and that the mass in her spleen was tiny. A sample had been sent off to find out what it was. She said that the portion of the liver that she could see looked healthy and that she was hopeful.

Chandi and I stayed with Pepper all night; she was incredibly uncomfortable after her surgery. We were sent home the next morning after a sleepless night, and slowly over the next couple of days Pepper started to recover. She was doing amazingly well, but then the call came to say that the results were back: Pepper had splenic haemangiosarcoma – it was cancer. There was nothing to be done, and even if I had been given the option of chemotherapy for Pepper, I don't think I would have taken it. The vet thought Pepper would have about a year to live, and that was pretty much it.

I researched the condition straight away and put Pepper on every supplement I could think of. I tried every natural alternative treatment I could come up with and spent the majority of the prize money that Chandi and I had won a few months before desperately trying to get Pepper well. I had always paid such attention to her diet and only let her drink mineral water, and she had had regular blood tests, which were then sent to a holistic vet in America who was an expert in sorting out nutritional deficiencies, but despite all of this, my precious girl had cancer.

Pepper got stronger over the course of the next week and we started to go out for rides in the car and gentle walks once more as soon as she was able. She was happy and was charging around and loving life again. I felt happy watching her enjoying herself and it was lovely to see both dogs seemingly well. When Pepper was recovered from the surgery, and able to go for longer walks, we went to Stapeley Common one day, one of our favourite walks. I asked Pepper to come and do one tempis with me, and with her fur blowing in the breeze, and a massive grin on her face, she raced over to be by my side. With Pepper in position, I asked her if she was ready and we skipped side by side, taking huge strides filled with joy. As we moved down the path, I fixed every detail of her face and this precious moment permanently in my memory. Applauding wildly after we had skipped for many steps, Pepper galloped off, happy and full of life. As I watched her leave my side, I knew that we had skipped together for the last time.

Pepper's condition started to deteriorate just days

later and she was unable to walk very much. Chandi realized that Pepper was poorly and never once pushed in for a fuss; she was happy for me to give Pepper all my attention. Pepper had a high temperature and went off her food. She stopped eating entirely, despite me doing everything I could think of to tempt her, even feeding her from my own plate. After watching her decline further and taking her every day to sit in the sunshine in the hills where she had loved to walk, things took a turn for the worse on the fourth anniversary of Mum's death.

We had all got in the car in the morning to go into the hills and I had picked some flowers from my garden to take to Mum and Dad's graves. It was a beautiful warm day and Pepper was a little bit brighter than the day before, sitting up in the car looking through the window. After visiting Mum's grave, we drove to our usual spot and I took Pepper's bed out of the boot of the car. I gently lifted Pepper off the back seat, and before she went to lie down, we ambled really slowly a few yards along the grass and Pepper sniffed at all the interesting smells, while Chandi stayed close by both of us.

We spent the rest of the day just sitting together looking at the view. I talked about all the great times we had shared over the years and told Pepper over and over how much I loved her. Before it was time to go home, we got up and went for a tiny stroll on the grass. Pepper walked in front a little and then froze and wouldn't move. I caught her just before she fell to the ground. I could see that she was in pain.

I had promised Pepper that I wouldn't allow her to suffer and so I lifted her into the car and let Chandi jump in behind, then drove to the vet's surgery. Pepper died in my arms at 6.15 p.m. on 23 August 2007, the fourth anniversary of Mum's death, while the birds sang in the trees around us. Pepper's pain was over, but mine and Chandi's had just begun.

While a grave was dug in my garden close to the house, Chandi lay beside Pepper's body without moving for four hours. After she had watched Pepper's body being gently lowered into the ground with her favourite squeaky ball, she turned and walked slowly into the house and howled.

TEN

Chandi, Crufts Champion

That first morning, waking after a few hours of fitful sleep to a pillow drenched in tears and remembering Pepper was gone, was terrible. Chandi was asleep on the bed next to me, which became her permanent place at night from that day onwards. I was wide awake and I clearly heard the sound of claws downstairs on the laminate flooring in the living room. It sounded as though there was a dog running around downstairs! With Chandi beside me and no one else in the house, it had to have been my angel Pepper showing me that she was fine and still with us in spirit.

Other times over the years I've heard her collar jingle when I've been in the garden and Chandi has been in the house lying in her bed. I've never seen Pepper, but I believe that she is close by.

Likewise, a few days after my mum died, four years earlier, I had been about to go outside, with my hand on the door handle, when a tiny white feather floated down from the ceiling right in front of my face and landed on my foot. I looked up in amazement to see where it had come from. There was no rational explanation for the feather, but I have since learned that some people believe a white feather is a sign that an angel is nearby and watching over you.

Numb from the shock of losing Pepper just four weeks after her diagnosis, I was floundering and the combined grief of the last seven years knocked me sideways. Chandi was also struggling in the weeks after Pepper's death. Chandi had been devoted to Pepper from the first moment they met. Pepper would sometimes feel sick during the night, and when she did, Chandi would come over to my bed and rest her chin on the mattress to wake me up. I'm a light sleeper, but if it didn't work, she would lift her chin and put it down harder. The first time it happened, I remember waking thinking she wanted a cuddle and crossly waving her away, but she didn't go. She stood her ground despite my cross words until I realized Pepper was being sick and rushed over to help her. I never ignored Chandi again and she told me every single time Pepper felt ill.

After Pepper died, Chandi stopped eating and it took quite a while for her to start eating on her own again without me having to hand-feed her. When Chandi thought I wasn't watching, she would go and stand next to Pepper's grave with her head bowed close to the ground. I knew just how she felt.

Chandi and I became even closer than ever. We only had each other now and we were constant companions. The howling that had been her forte in those early days after I'd brought her home from the dog pound had started again, and if the kitchen door closed on her when I wasn't there, she would howl in the most pitiful way. After attaching a rope to the door handle and showing Chandi how to open the door by pulling on it, she was able to get to me even if the door was shut.

I still went into school a couple of mornings a week to teach and there was no way I was prepared to leave Chandi distressed at home on her own. If I was away for more than a few minutes, she would not only howl but I would return to find her sitting bolt upright and shaking like a leaf. She had been fine to be left for those two mornings with Pepper, but with Pepper now gone, things had irrevocably changed. Teaching the rest of the time from home wasn't a problem, as Chandi would happily sleep in her bed in the next room if she could hear me talking and knew I was close by.

I considered leaving my job – in my current state of mind I really didn't care much about it anyway – but instead decided to sneak Chandi into school, hoping no one would notice. I was usually one of the first teachers to arrive, so there was a chance it might work. Chandi would sit concealed in a dog crate somewhere, and when lessons were finished, I could quickly take her out of the side gate to the car before returning for my things and leaving by the usual exit.

The music room at school was a tiny, dingy affair with a single window so high up on one wall that it was impossible to see out of it. With a mustard-yellow swirly patterned carpet, a door painted bright pink and the unmistakable smell of damp, it was not a pleasant room to be in for any length of time, so I was glad only to be there twice a week. I set the crate up next to the cupboard on the far side of the piano. With my chair in between the crate and my pupil sitting on the piano stool, no one actually noticed and we got away with it for three mornings. None of the children even realized that she was in the room, as Chandi was as quiet as a mouse. She sensed, I think, that we couldn't broadcast her presence there. Someone must have seen us going into school together, though, as on the fourth morning the headmistress asked to see me.

Chandi was without question my main concern and I felt my only choice was going to be to hand in my notice. I had never considered asking for permission to bring

Chandi in, because I was certain the headmistress would say no, so I was genuinely surprised when, instead of a reprimand, she told me she knew what I'd been doing and she was happy to let me continue. I didn't have to hide it any more. I was relieved.

Chandi got to accompany me every Monday and Wednesday, and would lie on her bed inside the crate and sleep. The only noises she occasionally made were some very loud snoring, much to the amusement of the children, and now and again a heavy sigh when she heard the same mistake repeated over and over again until the child perfected the bar we were working on. We were still grieving over our loss, but at least we were together.

There was one last opportunity to qualify for the following year's Crufts, but feeling completely despondent, we didn't go to the qualifying event and so there was to be no Crufts for us in 2008. I didn't care, though. Chandi and I spent our free time going out on walks or curled up together on the sofa, both of us desperately missing Pepper.

March 2008 arrived and Crufts came and went. I decided that Chandi and I couldn't just give up on everything we had worked so hard to achieve. After all, Pepper had started this amazing journey with me and I felt we owed it to her to see how far it would lead Chandi and me. With that in mind, we entered a qualifying competition to be held in April for the following year's Crufts and hastily threw a Freestyle routine together. I had a better idea in mind, but I wanted to save it for the actual final at Crufts if we managed to qualify.

The routine we prepared for the qualifying event wasn't very good, and I knew it, and in truth we hadn't even rehearsed it much. I was extremely nervous in the ring at the qualifying show, so much so that midway through the routine, my mind went blank and I couldn't remember any of the moves that made up the entire middle section. Neither could Chandi, as she didn't know it well enough either. We improvised and Chandi went along with me. I was relieved when I could at last remember what came next and we ended the routine as I had planned.

Despite everything, we came second and qualified for the Crufts Freestyle semi-final that was to be held the following January. We entered another show in June and also qualified for the Heelwork to Music class, in first place, for the Crufts Heelwork to Music semi-final.

Semi-finals had been introduced to the Crufts qualifying system that year due to the growing popularity of Heelwork to Music and Freestyle. We now had to compete and place in the top three in an initial show to qualify for a semi-final, and then also place in the top ten at the semi-final to qualify for the final, held a few weeks later.

Needing to find things to occupy us both, I also decided to fill in the entry form for the third series of *Britain's Got Talent*. I wasn't hopeful that our entry would even be considered given the amount of other television we had done over the last couple of years; I was concerned that Chandi and I had gained too much exposure with the BBC One talent show, *Richard and Judy* and *Blue Peter*, but I filled in the form online and hit send. Months later, we were sent a letter inviting us to audition in our first-choice location, Birmingham, at the end of October.

This was good news, but in the time between filling in the form and the letter arriving, a problem arose. Chandi was limping a little each time she got out of bed after resting. This had been going on for weeks, and despite going to the vet, having acupuncture and visiting the chiropractor, no one could find the cause of the problem. Someone suggested that Chandi had arthritis, but I wasn't so sure; once she had taken a couple of steps, she was then as sound as a bell. Of course I was worried about her, and, on the vet's advice, rested her completely for a fortnight. I slept on the sofa downstairs so Chandi wouldn't have the stairs to climb to be with me at night.

The rest didn't have the slightest effect: she was still lame after having basically sat in her bed, as good as gold, for two long weeks.

Things persisted but didn't get any worse. I was beside myself as I couldn't stand the thought of her being in pain. Then one day I noticed that she also limped when she was walking on the pebbles at the top of my garden. I went over to her and lifted her front paw to examine it. In all this time no one had looked at Chandi's paws, and as I examined it properly, I could see a huge split on the side of the big pad. No wonder it hurt when she was walking on the pebbles! It would have been uncomfortable when she first put her paw on the ground and put pressure on it after getting out of bed. She must have adjusted to the discomfort after a few steps.

By this time the *Britain's Got Talent* audition had come and gone; I could never ask Chandi to perform with a limp. After a few weeks of applying moisturizing balm to her pad, however, her paw healed and the limp disappeared.

In October, I was looking forward to meeting my friend Kayce Cover in person for the first time. She was coming over from America to Wood Green Animal Shelter, near Cambridge, to run a training course for her Syn Alia

Training System – SATS for short. I had first heard of Kayce just over five years before, when one of the top US Freestylers emailed me to ask if I used something called Bridge and Target training with Pepper and Chandi. I hadn't heard of it, but as usual Google came up trumps and delivered me to Kayce's website. I took a brief look but was overwhelmed by the amount of information and technical training terms I wasn't familiar with and didn't explore it further. This was a couple of months before Mum died, when I had so much else to occupy my mind. I forgot all about it and didn't revisit Kayce's website until four years later. Once I had started to explore her training methods, I was keen to learn more and so I emailed Kayce and sent off the small payment for the training manual she advertised. About an hour later, Kayce replied.

'Are you the Tina Humphrey who does the amazing Freestyle routines?'

It turned out that she had watched tapes of the UK competitions run by Rugby Dog Training Club and recognized my name from them!

Later that day, we phoned each other and spoke for the first time, and that was the start of our friendship. We hit it off instantly and I knew straight away that Kayce would become a good friend. That day, we spoke for over four hours and many phone conversations have since followed. I always look forward to speaking to her, and though we live in different countries, we continue to build a lasting friendship.

Kayce works with all kinds of animals, including dogs, horses and marine mammals. That first time we spoke, Kayce told me about her system of training, and the more she told me about her SATS method, the more I realized that what I had been instinctively doing with Chandi and Pepper was very similar. The 'tuh, tuh, tuh, tuh' sound I used to help and encourage Chandi to extend her passage movement when training for our dressage routine was the same as the part of Kayce's method called an Intermediate Bridge.

This Intermediate Bridge supports and gives the animal feedback while learning, and it is surprising that so few people are familiar with it or use it. The technique is based on the same principle as the children's game 'hot and cold', when you say, 'Warm . . . warm . . . warmer,' and so on, to guide the child to where he or she needs to be. Similarly, while working with an animal, you can vary the pitch and intensity of your voice when making a single-syllable sound to give the animal constant information and feedback so it can track its progress and be supported in its efforts. This continuous stream of information means that the animal doesn't have to guess at what is required or feel frustrated.

This is only one part of Kayce's method, but her whole system resonated on every level with me. The work I did with Pepper and Chandi had always been more than just training for competition; we lived and breathed our relationship, and I was always finding opportunities to teach them both about the world around us. I wanted our relationship to be based on mutual respect, understanding and communication, and it appeared that Kayce's philosophy was the same. I was amazed to realize that the way I had been working was similar to Kayce's incredible SATS method, which truly works with the intelligence of an animal.

I was excited to meet Kayce in person for the very first time. She flew from her home in Norfolk, Virginia, to the UK and Chandi and I drove to Cambridgeshire to see her. She had a free weekend before she started her training course at Wood Green Animal Shelter.

Meeting Kayce for the first time, it felt to me as though we were old friends. I was, and still am, very much in awe of her achievements working with exotic animals and the whole SATS method, which is so much more than just a training method. It is a new way to interact and communicate with the animals in your life. Kayce told me about the two-way communication she was working on with her horse and I was intrigued to find out more. She explained that among other things, she had taught her horse to be able to answer 'yes' or 'no' to a question, and gave me the idea to try it with Chandi. I also decided to teach Chandi more words. Chandi's vocabulary was already vast, but I was keen to increase it.

After my inspirational weekend with Kayce, I set about teaching Chandi the name of everything we encountered, from lamp-posts to rocks and trees.

'Can you show me a tree, Chandi?'

Chandi ran to the nearest tree and slapped her right front paw on it, while fixing me with a look that said, 'Have you forgotten what a tree is, Mum? Don't worry, I'll show you.'

'Can you show me a rock?'

Chandi looked around and placed her front paw on a rock that she liked the look of.

'Can you show me a gate?'

Chandi ran to the gate and touched it with her paw.

'Come on! Let's jump in the leaves!'

Chandi beat me to it, scooping her nose under the leaves and scattering them in the air to gently fall to the ground.

'Look! Squirrel! Quick, look up. Look up the tree!'

Chandi looked up and her eyes locked onto the squirrel. 'Chandi, there's a boy on a bike coming behind you. Can you look left?'

Chandi swung her head round to the left and spotted the bike.

'Let's stand still for a minute and let the bike go past.'

Chandi was often startled by joggers or cyclists coming up behind us when we were out walking. By expanding her vocabulary, she would never have to be caught off guard because I could tell her what was coming. She appreciates the information, and it's so easy to give it to her, and means that we can really communicate. When something has a name and an explanation attached, it isn't so scary.

Chandi used to be frightened of drains in the road. She would never walk on one, preferring to give it an exceptionally wide berth, and who can blame her? Any kind of monster could be living down there ready to grab her paw as she walked over it. Once I'd taken the time to name it 'drain' and show her that it was just water down there, she no longer avoided walking over one. Of course, the majority of the world's dogs get by without having the workings of a drain explained to them, but maybe it would make their lives better in some small way if they were offered an explanation.

In my kitchen, a food tray lives in its own designated space next to where Chandi eats. If I just grab the tray while she's eating, she springs back because I startle her.

If I say, 'Chandi, I'm just going to get my tray,' and then grab it, she doesn't move an inch. For me not to tell her now is rude and inconsiderate, and I am very keen to offer more information than ever before and explain everything to her.

Chandi doesn't particularly like swallowing her vitamin and mineral capsules, but she will do it. I show them to her, ask her if she'll swallow her pills and then ask her to get ready. She will open her mouth slightly and let me gently open it further and place the capsules at the back of her throat. She then swallows. I do this for each pill and always wait until she's ready and tells me so.

I said before that these ideas are simple, but they have made such a profound difference to Chandi's life. There is a growing band of people worldwide who live and work with their animals in the ways I do, and I owe a grateful debt of thanks to my dear friend Kayce Cover, who opened my eyes even further to the intelligence of dogs.

The increase in Chandi's vocabulary also meant that I could start working on the system of two-way communication I was so excited to hear about from Kayce. I set about showing Chandi how she could indicate 'yes' and 'no' by touching either my thumb or index finger, and then I started asking her simple questions such as 'Is this a tree?' while pointing to a tree. Chandi soon got the idea and was keen to tell me the correct answer. For example, if I point to a tree and ask her if it's a rock, I get the unequivocal answer: 'No!'

We quickly progressed to other questions, such as whether she wants to put her coat on or take it off, whether she wants me to open a gate for her and whether she wants to go for a walk. I have lost count of the number of words and names of tricks that Chandi knows – it's hundreds, and she only needs to be shown something a couple of times before she understands.

As well as touching the appropriate finger or thumb corresponding to her choice of 'yes' or 'no', Chandi's body language also speaks volumes. I know which answer she is going to give before she indicates it. If she wants to tell me 'yes', she gets excited and starts bobbing up and down on her front paws. If the answer is 'no', the reaction is subdued.

Having long studied Chandi's body language, I feel she has always communicated with me effectively, but this took things to a new level and gave her more freedom and control over her life. She gets a choice in the direction we take when we are walking now. When I first started offering her a say, she was very unsure and didn't seem comfortable. After some encouragement, she realized I really wanted her input and she tentatively started to make her own choices. I watched her confidence grow with every subsequent decision she made.

Now, when there is a choice of paths, I ask her which way she wants to go – right, left or straight on – and she will step forward onto the path going in the direction she has chosen and turn to look at me. On the one occasion I said that I didn't want to go in her chosen direction and headed down another path, her reaction brought me up short. She stood still, ears up, staring at me and wouldn't come onto my path. In no uncertain terms she was telling me she wanted to go her way. I felt humbled and a little embarrassed. Why had I asked her opinion, only to override it? I had no right to do that. From that point on, I reminded myself that if I didn't want to know the answer, I wouldn't ask the question.

It was a week after our lovely weekend with Kayce that Chandi started to scratch. In fact she scratched herself so badly that she tore out chunks of her own fur and was unable to stop even when her skin was bleeding. The vet wasn't sure what it was – perhaps an allergy or a parasite.

I had some routine blood tests done to see if they showed anything and I was horrified to see that her lipase, the enzyme produced by the pancreas, was horrendously high. Aside from her painful skin condition, I could see

Chandi didn't feel well, as she was less keen on running around out on a walk and, unusually, preferred to take it slowly. The only time she seemed truly happy was when I asked her if she wanted to do some heelwork or practise a few tricks, and then her ears would go up and her eyes would shine as she quickly got into position.

High levels of lipase could be due to pancreatitis, but she didn't show any obvious signs. The vet also thought it could be pancreatic cancer, which couldn't be treated. She suggested I take Chandi for a scan to investigate, but it would involve her having a general anaesthetic, which carries a risk, and if the cancer was untreatable there seemed little point, so I refused. The vet sent us home with a homeopathic remedy for the pancreas, which might help lower the lipase, but nothing for the scratching.

I did some research and found a natural product called Wobenzym that was designed to help the body deal with inflammation and might address the lipase level. Over the next eight months, Chandi would obligingly swallow huge doses of these pills three times a day – our close relationship and all our hours of training were vital for this. If Chandi had refused to swallow the vast quantity of pills she needed to take every day, we would have been scuppered. Every month when I took her back to the vet to check the lipase level, it had slowly decreased, but was still at a shockingly high level.

Chandi continued to scratch for weeks and I constantly had to stop her from tearing herself to shreds. I did some research of my own and started reading about a parasite called the sarcoptes mite, which is highly contagious for dogs and people. I made another appointment, and when we got to the surgery, I went in on my own and told the nurse in reception what I thought it was. She agreed that I shouldn't bring Chandi in case I was right and we infected another dog.

A blood test confirmed my suspicions. I was upset that the possibility of a parasitic infection hadn't been followed up before. As well as being contagious, it's a condition that gets worse the longer you leave it untreated!

I suddenly remembered meeting a man with three dogs when we were out on a walk a couple of months earlier, one of which had run over to Chandi. I remember thinking that it looked ill, with red skin and patches of fur missing. I was quick to get Chandi as far away from this dog as possible, but it would seem the infection had already been passed on.

The only treatment on offer was a parasite-killing medication to be applied to Chandi's skin, but the vet told me that it may not work as parasites were becoming resistant to these habitually abused preventative medications.

I have never used any parasite-control medication on Chandi, as she never routinely picks up fleas and I don't like to subject her to the unnecessary burden of chemicals or their side effects. Refusing the treatment, I decided to try neem oil instead, a natural solution I read about that could be used to kill the mites. For the next six weeks I bathed Chandi in neem oil mixed with shampoo at least once and usually twice or three times a day. It was back-breaking to wash her and dry her that many times each day and trying to work as well. Combined with bathing Chandi, every day I had to wash and dry everything that she lay on, as the mite can live and breed in the environment. My electricity bill was enormous, as I was doing two loads of washing each day and then using the tumble-dryer to help kill any remaining mites. The days were very long, and Chandi continued to scratch, but we persevered. The Crufts semi-finals for both Heelwork to Music and Freestyle were looming, and if Chandi wasn't better by then, we wouldn't be able to compete and I really wanted to, as we had two fantastic routines simmering away ready for the finals.

These months were incredibly stressful. I was fighting for Chandi's health, not prepared to just sit back and let whatever was making her ill just take its course. I had to stay awake each night to physically prevent Chandi from scratching at her skin until it bled. Eventually, the treatment for the parasites started to work and Chandi and I began to sleep at night again.

Chandi recovered from the sarcoptic mange just a few days before the Crufts semi-finals, and although her fur, which was missing in places where she had ripped it out scratching, hadn't started to grow back, we had the all clear to compete. Because her lipase was so elevated, though, I knew that Chandi still didn't feel very well.

Training for a few minutes each day, however, we were both happy. After Pepper died, I believe it was working with me on Freestyle practice that saved Chandi's life, as she had refused to eat for three weeks. The only thing I could think of was to take her food and go out to do some training. Training excited her; she loved it. When she did something I asked, I would feed her. She so loved her training that she didn't realize she was eating her dinner; she thought she was getting treats for a job well done. After three weeks of this, Chandi slowly started to show an interest in other things and began to eat from her plate once more.

For the Freestyle semi-final competition, we had decided to use the same routine that we had qualified with back in April, knowing that it was nowhere near our usual standard. An exciting new ballet-themed Freestyle routine I had planned for the Crufts final was to be kept under wraps until March, to give it the most possible impact.

As long as we came in the top ten in both the Freestyle and the Heelwork to Music semi-finals, it was good enough and was all we had to do to qualify for the Crufts finals. I had thought carefully about whether we should keep fighting to get to the competition – I was worried about Chandi's health and was absolutely exhausted from the months of back-breaking work bathing and drying Chandi multiple times a day, plus trying to prevent her from scratching herself to pieces during the night. The endless worry of seeing my precious girl in such a state did nothing to help either. Chandi had been so uncomfortable for so long now, and with the elevated lipase she really didn't feel very well. But a voice in my head kept saying over and over: This is not how our story is supposed to end.

I was compelled to carry on, and Chandi enjoyed working on the new routines, despite feeling poorly. I decided that as she was not stressed at competitions, it made no difference if we at least tried to get through to the finals: she would enjoy herself, and it might take her mind off everything else. With the vastly elevated lipase level hanging over us, and the cause still unknown, I was aware that this could be our last competition together, and I wanted to walk out on that green carpet one last time with Chandi prancing by my side.

We did our best at the semi-finals and managed to qualify in second and fourth place for the Heelwork to Music and Freestyle finals respectively, which was good enough. Now we had six weeks to prepare for the big Crufts final. I hoped that if Chandi continued to take the Wobenzym, the lipase level might fall even further. My bank balance was decreasing pretty quickly, as I was spending £98 every eight days on tablets for Chandi, putting what remained of the prize money from winning *When Will I Be Famous?* to good use once more. Without that money, I don't know what I would have done.

The weeks leading up to Crufts went very quickly, training and working on our ballet-themed Freestyle routine. As always, I had left the finer details of the routine until the last moment, and although I had a rough idea of the choreography and had chosen the music, I still needed to get hold of a portable ballet barre and put a costume together. I found a barre online and, when it arrived, set it up in the living room so we could practise with it indoors.

The ballet barre was going to set the scene for the whole routine and get the audience hooked right from the word go. I put a story together for the performance: I was to be dressed as the cleaner of the ballet studio, with a broom in my hand at the start of the routine. Chandi would play the ballet professional and, seeing that I was curious, would show me how to do some ballet moves. As always I wanted to have something belonging to my mum in the ring with me, so I chose an old blue-painted broom to use as my prop.

Near the start of the routine, Chandi and I stand side by side at the barre, me with my hands resting on it, Chandi her front paws. She then lifts first her left hind leg, then her right; I see what she is doing and copy her. We worked for ages on this move, teaching Chandi that her leg lifts had to match mine.

Next, Chandi performs a move that I had had in my head for eight years – I wear a scarf with cleaner's over-alls and Chandi removes them both to reveal a ballet costume underneath. I showed Chandi how to grab the end of the scarf with her mouth and then run backwards with it, stand on her hind legs and turn round so the scarf would transfer from being wrapped round my neck to being wrapped round hers!

This move caused me endless worries, because I knew that she was going to be hot in the arena and it was going to be difficult for her to remember not to pant. If she forgot, she would drop the scarf and the move would be ruined. We practised it countless times and finally she learned to hold the scarf firmly in her mouth until the move was complete.

Props are a double-edged sword. They can create magic in a routine, but they can also seriously backfire. Using three props in this routine – a broom, a barre and a scarf – was risky, but I knew Chandi was capable of doing everything just as we had planned. We worked on all the minute details, with me trying to foresee every problem that could happen, and to think of a solution so I wouldn't be left stranded in the ring if things went awry.

Working with Chandi was the easy bit; working with the broom was a nightmare! I swear it had a life of its own, and trying to move while holding it in the different positions the choreography called for was fraught with danger. I don't think I've ever fallen over so much while rehearsing a routine or whacked myself in the head so many times. Chandi knows that if anything happens during a routine, she is supposed to just carry on. She completely understands what we are doing and keeps going no matter what. She will continue even if I accidentally tread on her paw, bash into her or swing a broom dangerously close to her head. Eventually I did get the hang of dancing with the broom; either that or the broom decided to cooperate a little more!

The story of the routine continues with me becoming

more proficient at ballet the more we dance. I included our back-to-back move, which looked stunning in this setting, and the routine ends with a series of fast hind-leg moves and a bow to one another. I was so excited about this new routine, and knew from the goosebumps on my arms when I ran it through in my head that it had the potential to please the audience at Crufts and, hopefully, the judges too. If this was to be our last ever Freestyle routine, I wanted it to be memorable.

The first day of Crufts dawned, and having qualified for both the Freestyle and the Heelwork to Music finals, we had two days of competition to look forward to. The furthest thing from my mind was the possibility of having to return for a third day to compete in the international Freestyle competition, which was the fate of the winner of the Freestyle final.

Roy kindly came with us again, bringing his sack truck trolley to help us get all the props into the arena. These included the portable ballet barre, which was quite long and very heavy, a chair and Mum's blue-painted broom, along with my costume, food, collapsible crate and Chandi's bed. I got up that day at 5.30 a.m., bleary-eyed but excited, to await Roy's arrival. We arrived at the Crufts venue bright and early at 8 a.m. on the first day.

The competition was now in the huge main arena,

with a seating capacity of many thousands, much bigger than anywhere we'd performed before. We had ages to wait, but this meant I had time to get settled, change into my costume and warm up Chandi. We had a running order of nine out of ten competitors, which was excellent but meant that we had even longer to wait before it was our turn in the ring.

From where we were benched, we could hear roars of appreciation from the audience during the other routines, and there was a huge monitor showing what was happening in the arena. There was no sound, but the pictures looked amazing – with action replays of the best parts while the scores were decided and fed into the computer for display on the huge scoreboard.

I was feeling very emotional and tears started to run down my face. I didn't know what was wrong with Chandi – her lipase had only fallen a few points that month and was still horrendously high. I didn't know if this was to be our last competition together or what was in store for us over the next few months. We were making more special memories, though, and the time we had together was precious.

We made our way down to the arena during competitor number seven's routine. Roy was already there working out where to place the ballet barre and the chair so the judges could get the best view of our movements during the routine.

The ballet barre was an absolute nightmare to set up. The four legs pulled out and needed to be completely extended to be made rock steady. This was the difficult part, because as one leg was extended, the position of the others seemed to shift, and each leg needed checking many times. If it wasn't fixed and stable, when Chandi jumped up to land her front paws on it, it would wobble and this would throw her off. I couldn't afford for anything to go wrong, certainly nothing that could be avoided, so Roy was under pressure.

Finally it was our turn. I watched out of the corner of my eye as Roy and the steward ran into the arena to set everything up while the audience was waiting for the scores for the previous competitor. I continued to warm up Chandi and keep her focused on me. She was excited about being in the arena and keen to get started. The atmosphere was electric, and the crowd were making a tremendous amount of noise in support of each competitor.

Roy put everything in the right place and, after checking them repeatedly, did a brilliant job of getting the barre legs solid and stable. He turned and ran out of the ring, puffing out his cheeks and wishing me luck as Chandi and I were announced. I looked at Chandi and she looked up at me.

'Well, this is it, kid,' I said, and bent down to kiss her head. She turned to lick the side of my face and then got into position by my left side. Taking a deep breath, I asked her if she was ready and we set off into the ring, Chandi doing her most impressive floating-on-air trot and looking stunning.

Chandi pranced across the arena to the far side where the props were set up and, asking her to wait a short distance away from the chair, I went to sit down and open up my newspaper for the start of the routine. Chandi watched for me to cue the music by nodding my head. The music started and off we went. As I was putting my newspaper down, Chandi played her part in the story beautifully, leading the way to the barre and looking back to see if I was keeping up. She jumped up on her hind legs on cue and landed her front paws on the barre, which was rock steady, thanks to Roy. Lifting up her left hind leg and holding it in the air until I asked her to lift her right hind leg, she was flawless. I joined in with the movements and we were perfectly in time. I heard the audience laugh in response.

Next Chandi grabbed my sleeve and pulled off my overalls. She caught hold of it in her teeth and gave it an almighty yank, while I twirled round so fast I nearly lost my balance. She dropped the sleeve and grabbed the end of the scarf as I asked her to go back and up on her hind legs. Chandi clamped her jaws tightly on the scarf and didn't let go until it was wound beautifully round her neck. We went into the back-to-back pirouette, which was greeted with the applause I had hoped for, and we kept going, building up to the finale.

It was all over in a flash. We had finished and every single move had gone according to plan. The audience had even laughed and clapped in all the right places. Taking time to stop and savour the moment, I told Chandi to take a bow while the audience applauded. I joined in with the applause for Chandi, in no hurry to leave the ring. Chandi was so excited and was running round me with her tail furiously wagging. We bowed together to each side of the arena and then ran to the exit and back to the collecting ring. I gave Chandi a drink of water out of her bowl, a few pieces of cheese and a huge cuddle.

I could see a camera coming up behind me to film us; the competition was being broadcast for the first time live over the Internet. I turned my back on the camera as tears were now pouring down my face. I was so delighted with how things had gone for us, and for those few minutes in the ring I had forgotten that there was anything wrong with Chandi. Reality had hit me, though, as we left the ring, and I didn't want anyone to know that I was crying – only a few people knew that Chandi was poorly and I wanted it to stay that way.

While I was hugging her, I heard the scores being announced in the background and the commentator say, '. . . and Tina and Chandi go into the lead!'

The audience erupted in response and I hugged Chandi even closer. There was one more team left to compete and I dared not even hope that we might hold on to the lead. Five minutes later, the final result was announced: Chandi and I had won our second Crufts title!

All ten finalists filed into the arena for the awards ceremony. The main arena lights went out and there was a spotlight just on me and Chandi. I suddenly felt self-conscious. I crouched down next to Chandi as it was announced officially that we had won the competition. We were called forward and presented with a huge green Crufts rosette and a beautiful cut-glass trophy engraved with the Crufts logo.

When the second-place team, John Higginbottom and Ivy, had been awarded their trophy, John stepped back to stand by me and said, 'This is a moment you'll remember all your life.'

I couldn't reply as I was too choked with tears, so I just smiled back and bent down to stroke Chandi and share the moment with her. Music started to play and it was our job to lead the lap of honour all the way round the huge arena. Instead of walking, Chandi and I looked at one another and she read my mind; we both started to skip, with me waving shyly to the crowd as we did, in acknowledgement of their applause.

Still glowing from our win, we left the ring and I made Chandi comfortable in her bed, putting a huge blanket over the top so she was hidden from the crowds of people filing past out of the main arena. After quickly changing out of my costume and finding both of us something to eat, I curled up on the bench next to her and closed my eyes. Chandi would only sleep if she knew I was next to her, so I stayed there, reliving the morning's events over and over in my mind. As the winners of the competition, we were scheduled to do our routine once more in the main arena at around 5 p.m., this time under four huge spotlights. Also, as winners of the Freestyle final, we would represent England in the international Freestyle final on Saturday. It was a long and tiring day, but the effort and struggle had been worth it. We had to do it all over again tomorrow, though, as we had qualified for the Heelwork to Music final as well.

Chandi and I set off back to Crufts on our own the next day and made our way back to the same bench. I loved our Heelwork routine. I knew from the first moment I heard the song on the radio that it was perfect for what I wanted to create. The words so accurately described my relationship with Chandi and our dedication to each other during all the struggles that we had been going through, both in the past and right now. The song was Leona Lewis's 'Footprints in the Sand'.

Again we were performing ninth out of ten teams. With no props to worry about, Chandi and I sat quietly thinking about our routine. We made our way down to the arena and warmed up in a corner of the collecting ring.

When it was our turn, and the commentator announced us, I asked Chandi if she was ready. We made our way into the huge arena, Chandi by my side, head thrown back and front legs prancing high in her beautiful exaggerated trot. We stopped, turned to face the judges, took a deep breath, nodded for the music to start and began.

The moves flowed freely and Chandi performed every one accurately. Our legs matched in height for the Spanish Walk and we moved in unison. Chandi floated through the transitions from trot to one tempis and then into the sideways work. We sailed through into the next section and on into our back-to-back move, which was greeted by applause from the audience. There were more sideways movements as we made huge fluid sideways leaps. It felt as though we were flying through the air.

We held the audience in the moment after the music

came to an end and then stood up to acknowledge their reaction. It was good! Once more everyone in the arena, including me, applauded Chandi. We took a final bow, delighted it had gone so well, then left the ring to await our scores.

Chandi and I headed back to a peaceful, dark corner just outside the collecting ring and sat quietly together, waiting for the final routine to finish and the overall result to be announced. My mind was racing – no dog had ever won both Crufts Freestyle and Heelwork to Music finals in the same year. Were we to set a record here or be pipped to the post?

Suddenly it was time to find out, as the final scores were in. Chandi and I were still sat together on the floor away from the harsh glare of the lights. My heart started to beat faster and then the whole world seemed to come to a standstill as they announced the winners. It was us! We had done it again, setting a record. I was so pleased, and so deliriously proud of Chandi.

After the awards ceremony, we went straight back to the benches for a rest – I know I was exhausted and felt completely drained, and despite the joy she displayed whenever we did well, I knew Chandi was tired too. We had to give another performance after 5 p.m. under the spotlights, making it a second long day.

That evening performance under the spotlights was

very special and I will always treasure the memory. Pepper was never far from my thoughts that day, and when asked, before we began, whether I had anything to say, I dedicated the performance to the memory of my beautiful Pepper, who was sadly there only in spirit. Peter Purves, who was doing the commentary for the live stream over the Internet, read my dedication as Chandi and I proudly walked into the ring. The video was later uploaded to YouTube and watched by thousands.

Afterwards, we wearily made our way back to the benches to pack our things before heading home. Many people making their way out of the arena were coming up to congratulate us and confiding that they had found our routine incredibly moving.

When we got back to the car park, we both just sat staring ahead for a few minutes, stunned and shattered. I started to smile and Chandi leaned over to rest her head on my shoulder and lick my face. As I started the engine, Chandi sighed and went to sleep. We had another, final competition the following day for the international event and we needed all the rest we could get.

Chandi and I were at a distinct disadvantage for the third day of competition, having already done two full days at Crufts with long journeys each day. We were honoured to be representing England, though, and we happily dragged ourselves back to the Crufts venue once more, with Roy and our trolley full of the props needed for our ballet routine.

We were drawn third to last in the running order that day. Chandi performed wonderfully and only made one mistake, but I knew that just one mistake could potentially be very costly. We had done our best, though, and despite everything, we had given a good performance and had got a great reaction from the packed arena.

When the results came in, we were in the lead and we waited for the last few competitors to perform before hearing the final scores. We were tired but content and quietly enjoying the honour of being at Crufts for a third day in a row. Already flushed with success, we were happy just to be there, so when the final results were announced, we were completely overwhelmed: Chandi and I had won for the third time in three days!

We set two records that year at Crufts. Not only was Chandi the first dog to win both Heelwork to Music and Freestyle finals at the same Crufts, but with the international title she was now also the first dog ever to win all *three* finals in the same year – and is still the only dog to hold both these records. Together with winning the very first combined Heelwork to Music and Freestyle final back in 2005, Chandi now had a total of four Crufts titles to her name, two more than any other dog in the country. I couldn't have been more proud of my precious girl.

As on the other two days, we were asked to perform again in the main arena at the end of the day, but Chandi was just too tired, so the third-placed team had the honour. Meanwhile, Chandi and I shuffled home with another beautiful crystal trophy, a rosette and treasured memories of our unbelievable success.

ELEVEN

A New Adventure

In the days after Crufts, I couldn't help but think about what Chandi and I had achieved and what we had had to battle against just to take part in the finals, let alone win them. The loss of Pepper and ongoing worries about Chandi's health could so easily have held us back, but Chandi had matched me in my desire not to let our story end on a sad note – if it was soon going to end. We didn't give up when times got hard. Not only had Chandi shown that she wanted to continue training, but she had also taken great delight in performing twice a day in the main arena and gave her all in each and every performance. It wasn't until a few hours before the last spotlight performance on the third day that she told me she had done enough and I called time on Crufts 2009.

We continued to fight Chandi's elevated lipase after the all-consuming events of Crufts. Her blood tests showed a slow but steady decrease over the next six months. The level was still way above the normal range, but at least we were heading in the right direction. Hopefully she was feeling a little better. The Wobenzym pills continued to have a positive effect. I still had no idea what was actually causing the problem, but I tried hard not to dwell on the possibility of it being cancer and together we just enjoyed each and every day as much as possible. Chandi's energy level had decreased significantly and some days all she wanted to do was walk slowly by my side. I was happy to do whatever she wanted and made sure I kept to her pace. I never want her to feel 'old and useless', because in my eyes with each passing day she becomes more precious.

I continued to research possible causes of Chandi's elevated lipase and one day I came across a reference linking it to food allergies. I couldn't find anything else beyond that, but I decided to reassess Chandi's diet anyway. She had always eaten organic raw food, but I wondered if there was something she could be intolerant to. To see if diet was a contributing factor, I stopped giving her raw chicken and eggs one day in September and within three weeks I noticed a difference in Chandi's energy level. The difference was slight, but it encouraged me to keep going and I anxiously awaited the results from her next blood test after four weeks. It appeared that it had made a difference, as the lipase had plummeted and was almost within the normal range.

I have never fed Chandi chicken or eggs again, and with the oppressive worry no longer dominating my life and Chandi's energy level slowly increasing, I decided that it was very definitely time for another adventure. Chandi would turn eleven on 13 July that year, 2009. Having won every major Freestyle and Heelwork to Music competition many times over and set records at Crufts, I felt it was time for a new challenge.

I filled in the online application form for the fourth series of *Britain's Got Talent* and waited. Having spent years perfecting our craft at Freestyle shows around the country and being at the very top of the sport, I felt it really was time to have a go at moving things up a gear and doing something new and more inspiring. The opportunities that could arise from being on the biggest talent show on television seemed exciting, and Chandi and I were ready, having paid our dues and worked incredibly hard for nearly eleven years.

At the end of October, I was delighted to receive a letter from *Britain's Got Talent* inviting us to an audition in Birmingham on 14 December. I prepared a shorter version of our ballet routine. Three weeks before the audition, however, something else went wrong.

We had returned home from a walk in the pouring rain and Chandi, as usual, sat patiently in front of me, offering her front paws in turn for me to dry with her pawprint towel. When she passed me her left paw, though, I noticed some redness in between the pads. Taking a closer look, I could see a skin infection. We went to our vet, who gave me a combined antibiotic and steroid cream. I wasn't keen on giving Chandi steroids, but after trying a few alternatives, it was the only solution.

Worried about the infection but satisfied that we were addressing it properly, I thought we could focus on the audition, but it wasn't to be. After Chandi had eaten her dinner one evening and I was cleaning her teeth, I noticed, to my horror, that one tooth was not only missing a great chunk off the bottom, exposing the pulp, but the side was also sheared off and hanging in the gum. I immediately phoned the vet again. I knew what she'd say: the only option was to remove the tooth under general anaesthetic.

This happened just ten days before the audition and we hadn't even started rehearsing the routine. After Chandi's paw got a little better and she recovered from the dental work, we wouldn't have much time to perfect it.

The appointment had to be made, though, and after a very sleepless night, I took Chandi to the vet. She was given the pre-med injection while still in the car in order to keep her as calm as possible. I always worry terribly about general anaesthetics, all the more so the older Chandi gets. I know that there is always a chance that something may go wrong and my precious girl may not wake up again. I didn't want her to be frightened in a strange place, so, understanding my reasons, our vet got in the back of our car and injected Chandi while she was on the front seat, with me distracting her. I tried to comfort her as the drugs started to make her feel peculiar and talked to her before the sickening moment when she went limp. With Chandi unconscious, the tears I had held back now came rushing down my face as the veterinary nurses came to carry her into the operating theatre.

The surgery was not exactly straightforward: the tooth's deep roots meant they had to drill into it in sections. It left a gaping hole in Chandi's gum, which needed several stitches to close up. Fortunately it was soon over, and after sitting with her while the effects of the drugs wore off, we were told we could go home. I had been so stressed since finding the broken tooth in Chandi's mouth that I was exhausted and couldn't wait to get her home.

It didn't take her long to start to feel better, and her paw was improving quickly too. We were soon able to begin rehearsing our audition routine. I didn't want to get Chandi's foot dirty, so we practised on our driveway, much to the amusement of our neighbours and the postman, who would stop to watch us. As I knew from previous experience that the amount of space available to us in a TV audition could be extremely limited, we had no need to use our usual training area up in the hills. I dragged some large rubber-backed mats out of the garage and onto the drive so Chandi's foot would stay clean and dry. Setting up the ballet barre as well, we practised each morning, and thankfully the routine came together quickly, with Chandi as keen as ever to practise all the movements until they were perfect.

Audition day soon arrived and Roy was kind enough to come and help us once more with all the heavy props, including the practise mats, in case the audition room didn't have carpet. I had been assured there would be carpet, but I wanted to be prepared. It was too dangerous for Chandi to work on a slippery floor.

When we arrived at the NEC – the same venue as the recent Crufts finals – we were called in pretty quickly. I had asked if it was possible to be seen fairly soon so Chandi wasn't left hanging around in the packed 'holding room', and the organizers were good enough to oblige. There were two people auditioning before us, so I still had time to warm Chandi up before Roy, with the help of one of the researchers, went in to the audition room to lay the mats on the uncarpeted floor and set up the ballet barre. In the meantime, one of the *Britain's Got Talent* researchers introduced himself as Frankie. We had corresponded several times via email the previous year, when I had had to pull out of the audition because of Chandi's split paw pad. Frankie remembered us, even though we hadn't made it to that audition.

When the room was just about ready, the researcher beckoned to us to come in. Roy was making one final adjustment to the ballet barre, checking it was perfectly stable, and Chandi ran over and sat down directly in front of him, almost tripping him up as he turned to leave the room. Chandi had other ideas, and every time Roy moved to the side to get past her, Chandi as quick as a flash shuffled in the same direction and leaned into him, wanting to be stroked. Roy and I both started to laugh, and I quickly asked Chandi to come to me. Roy was slightly red in the face by this time and she finally let him leave the room so our audition could begin.

The room was set up in the same way it had been at every audition we had been to previously, with just one producer and a cameraman. After introducing ourselves to the producer sitting behind the desk, handing him our CD and saying hello to the cameraman, Chandi and I took up our starting position. The music began and off we went, every move of our shortened routine going pretty much according to plan. I was very relieved when it was over, though, as again I was uncomfortable performing with our audience of two being able to hear all my verbal cues to Chandi.

When it was over, the producer introduced himself as Ben and was very complimentary about Chandi. I mentioned that she was a rescue dog and that she had won a few things at Crufts.

After the audition, we spent an hour doing some filming with a small crew. We packed up all our props and went home when we were finished, Chandi sleeping as she always did. If we were successful in this audition, we would receive a phone call some time in January.

Christmas came, and for the first time since Mum had died, I decorated the house, feeling slightly more positive and marginally more festive than in previous years. Chandi and I spent Christmas on our own again, though. It was our second Christmas without Pepper. Chandi was very kind and attentive; she took me out for some lovely walks and then snuggled up with me on the sofa. I tried not to think about the audition or the phone call that probably wouldn't ever come, but it was impossible not to.

I was about to be given something to take my mind off it, though, as Chandi developed yet another problem that needed our vet's attention. She had had a polyp on her left leg since puppyhood, and though it had grown a bit over the years, it had never caused a problem . . . until now. Just before Christmas, a blister developed on the surface, which quickly turned into a sore that, despite my best efforts, would not heal.

It didn't bother Chandi, being on the outside of her leg, and I would keep a little bandage on it when we went out for walks. The only option the vet could suggest was to surgically remove it under yet another general anaesthetic. Chandi had only just had surgery for her broken tooth and I tried everything to avoid going through that again. I persevered, trying to get it to heal. As it wasn't hurting Chandi or affecting her in any way, there was no real urgency and the vet was happy for me to keep trying, but the possibility of another operation was hanging over me and I wondered if we'd have to go down that route.

In the middle of a piano lesson in early January, the phone rang. I don't usually answer the phone when I'm teaching, but this time I just felt I had to.

'Hello.'

'Hi. Can I speak to Tina, please?' asked the voice on the other end of the line.

'Speaking,' I replied.

'This is Oli from *Britain's Got Talent*. I'm just ringing to ask if you have a performing animal licence for Chandi.'

After a small, stunned pause from my end, I replied, 'Yes, I do have one.'

'OK, then, that's great, thanks. Bye.' And the phone went dead.

Blimey! What did that actually mean? I hadn't been told I was through to the next round, but why ask about a licence if we weren't through to the next round? Maybe they were covering all their bases and asking everyone with animals to get a licence before deciding who to put through. I didn't know what to think. After two days of this going round and round in my head, I couldn't stand it any more, so I emailed Frankie, the researcher, to ask what it had meant, not for one second expecting a reply. I received one about a minute later.

'All I can say is you've received a call from Oli already!'

My email back to him was short and to the point. 'Holy cow! Although I shall continue to hold my breath until someone says the actual words I need to hear!'

Again I received an almost instant reply. 'Yes, hold that breath until the call.'

Did that mean we were through? I was desperate to know! With nothing to lose and trying to be witty, I left it about five minutes and then wrote back, 'Any idea how long I'm going to have to wait for a call, because I'm rapidly turning blue?!'

Again he replied straight back. 'You should get a call in the next couple of days.'

Not knowing anything for definite, I decided that if the news was bad, Frankie wouldn't have answered me in the first place. Nevertheless, the anticipation and frustration of not truly knowing was agonizing, and I didn't know how much longer I could wait. Fortunately the call I had been longing for came the very next day. I spoke to David, the researcher who was to look after me and Chandi so well over the next five months, for the first time and he told us that we were through to the next round and would finally have our chance to audition in front of Simon Cowell, Amanda Holden and Piers Morgan. We were on the phone for over an hour and I was asked so many questions about myself and Chandi that by the time it was over, I was exhausted – but delighted!

The next round of auditions was being held in February back at the Hippodrome in Birmingham, where we had previously auditioned for the BBC One show *When Will I Be Famous?* I dragged the heavy mats out of the garage every day with the ballet barre, and Chandi and I practised our socks off, trying to ensure that the routine would again go to plan in a more stressful environment complete with judges and audience.

On the day of the audition, we struggled into the Hippodrome with our ballet barre and broom, past the crowds waiting to be admitted into the audience. We were taken up to a small room heaving with people in every type of costume imaginable and told that we were needed for an interview and some footage of us arriving. I dumped all our stuff in a corner and gave Chandi a drink, while the ballet barre was whisked off down to the stage, ready for our performance a little later on. I was looking forward to a few minutes to ourselves to relax, but no – two of the acts would shortly be doing an interview with Ant and Dec, who were presenting the show. We were being interviewed first, so we were told to stay where we were. As I sat there waiting, it all felt a little surreal waiting to speak to Ant and Dec. I had seen them on TV, of course, but how odd it was to know I would speak to them soon! I smiled to myself and shook my head in disbelief as all the incredible things Chandi and I had done together flashed through my mind. Chandi, thinking I was upset, put her front paw on my knee and leaned in close, always ready to comfort me.

Suddenly there was a cheer and I looked up to see Ant and Dec waving to everyone in the holding room. They headed in my direction and sat down next to us. While I was being interviewed, Chandi slapped her paw up onto Ant's knee and then leaned into Dec, grinning up at him.

With the interview over, it was time to be escorted down to the stage. As Chandi and I stepped out of the lift and opened the door to the backstage area, we could hear the famous buzzers going off and each time they did the floor shook so much that I could feel the vibration from my feet to my knees. I looked down at Chandi, worried that she wouldn't cope with this level of noise, as it was more extreme than anything either of us had heard before. She didn't bat an eyelid. She has been in so many different situations now that I don't think anything surprises her; she just expects weird things to happen and accepts it all. For me, though, it was incredibly unsettling and I suddenly wondered whether I had the courage to risk total humiliation if the audience hated our act. If I hadn't had Chandi by my side, there is no way I would have walked out onto the stage.

We were the fourth act of the afternoon show, and while we were waiting backstage, unable to focus on much other than the buzzers the judges used to buzz people off, I tried to warm up Chandi. She couldn't hear me talking to her because of the noise, though, and it was virtually impossible. Just then I felt the most nervous I have ever felt, as I wondered what I'd got us both into.

Suddenly we were told to get into position at the side of the stage ready to go on. It was our turn next. All the acts before us had received three buzzes from the judges, along with extremely uncomplimentary critiques and jeering from the audience. I was terrified. Chandi, thankfully, seemed fine.

I shuffled forward with her, keeping my hand on her shoulder to guide her as she couldn't hear me. I looked up and there was Dec, grinning at me. I politely offered him a piece of cheese from Chandi's pot of treats, but after pointing out that it was a bit sweaty, having been out of the fridge for several hours, he politely declined and we both giggled.

I looked out from the wings to see, to my absolute horror, that the ballet barre was on the stage but the legs hadn't been extended properly. I pointed it out to Dec, as he was the nearest person to me, and he told me that I would have time to see to it before we had to perform. I wasn't too reassured by this, as it was going to take me a while to sort out and the audience might be baying for blood by that stage. There was nothing to be done other than walk out on the stage with Chandi a few seconds later. Dec wished us luck as we stepped out into the glaring lights.

In the wings it was relatively calm, but as soon as we were on the stage the noise, lights and sheer energy created by the audience seemed to hit us. Both Chandi and I were temporarily stunned. With me stooping forward so I could walk with my hand lightly on Chandi's back – which, I confess, was more to comfort me than

Chandi – we walked to the microphone at the front of the stage and faced the judges. The lights were so strong that I couldn't see the audience, only the judges, and for that I was really grateful. Simon Cowell was absent, due to having man flu, which I've heard is the very worst possible kind of flu, and sitting in Simon's chair was none other than Louis Walsh, who proceeded to ask us who we were and what we were there to do.

'I'm Tina, and this is Chandi the Amazing Dancing Dog.'

I swear I could hear the audience's eyes roll back in their heads when they heard that Chandi was a dancing dog.

'Oh good,' replied Louis, drawing the words out slowly with distinct incredulity, 'a dancing dog. Off you go in your own time.'

Before we could start the routine, though, I had to sort out the legs of the ballet barre. I asked Chandi to lie down close to the barre and then proceeded to adjust the legs, going from one leg to the next and back again. After I'd been round it about six times, the audience were laughing at me and I was red with embarrassment. I could sense everyone in the theatre was thinking: We've got a right one here!

I glanced over to where I'd left Chandi and my heart lurched when she wasn't there. I stood upright and looked around. Chandi had got up and walked to the centre of the stage and was sitting bolt upright looking out at the audience, with her ears down. I caught her eye and smiled at her, and then in complete desperation shouted to the burly props guys who were standing in the wings watching me struggle, 'Please can someone help me?!'

At last someone walked out, grabbed one leg of the barre while I grabbed the opposite one and pulled. It was finally fixed in place and Chandi and I could do what we'd come to do.

I called Chandi, who was still sat in the middle of the stage. She didn't look happy – her ears were down on her head, and her eyebrows were knitted together – which only made the sinking feeling in my stomach worse. This wasn't how it was supposed to go! Despite a few attempts, she wouldn't look up at me, so, offering up a short prayer, I just asked her to get into the starting position, with one front leg crossed over the other at the barre. I nodded in Dec's direction for the music to start. As soon as Chandi saw me nod, her eyes locked on to mine and her whole mood seemed to lighten; her ears flicked up, and her eyebrows seemed to rise in anticipation. She was ready.

We did the leg-lifting sequence at the ballet barre near the start of the routine and I thought I heard a murmur of laughter from the audience. Then, with each move, the reaction seemed to get louder. I was so relieved and felt encouraged. Chandi kept working and everything went far better than I originally expected. When the music ended, Chandi and I took a bow, and I stayed bending down to stroke her and congratulate her as the applause started. Chandi was pleased it was over and was wagging her tail furiously, her whole body wiggling from side to side as I praised her. I didn't dare look up, I was so overwhelmed. Finally I couldn't stay in that position any longer, so I straightened up and looked out at the audience. My eyes had by now adjusted to the harsh lights and I could see the audience were on their feet, and so were Amanda and Louis – he was clapping like a seal with a huge grin on his face! It was quite a moment, and one I will never forget. The applause and standing ovation went on for ages, so Chandi and I took another bow. At last the audience quietened down and Piers gave his verdict.

'I'm not usually a fan of dog acts, but that is the best dog act we've ever had on the show!'

I was stunned and thanked him.

Amanda said, 'You can tell how much she wants to please you, to thank you for looking after her.'

Finally, it was Louis's turn to give his opinion.

'It was the best dog act I've ever seen!'

It was time for them to vote. I held my breath and

bent down to cuddle Chandi as Piers gave me a 'yes' and then went on to say, 'I'm so sorry Simon wasn't here to see that – he'd have loved it, so I'm giving you a "yes" from Simon as well.'

Amanda gave us another 'yes', and Louis rounded off their verdict: 'You've got *four* "yeses"!'

Ecstatic, and so relieved, Chandi and I took one final bow and walked off stage back into the wings, where Ant and Dec were waiting. Dec congratulated me, patted me on the back and bent down to stroke Chandi. With the next act waiting to go on stage, we were ushered away and Chandi and I went to sit in the darkest corner we could find to compose ourselves and try to understand what had just happened.

A week later, Chandi and I were to go to London for the filming of the 'reveal day', where the forty acts that had made it through to the live semi-finals would be announced. The night before, I was in such a panic as I just didn't know how I was going to manage what would undoubtedly be a long and exhausting day. I phoned my friend Debbie, who knew immediately that I was in a real state and tried to calm me down.

Debbie worked at the school where I taught the piano and we'd known each other to say 'hello' to for years. A year or so before, however, still reeling from the loss of

Pepper, I had started talking to her in the corridor and discovered we shared a love of dogs. Debbie understood my devotion to Chandi like no one had ever understood before. From then on, I would always go to find Debbie to have a chat, and she had become a good and close friend.

Deb and I have a lot in common and I'm so grateful that we spoke to each other that day, otherwise I'd have missed out on a wonderful friendship. I feel we understand each other, and we share the same wicked sense of humour.

Thankfully she came to the rescue that day when we spoke. Deb knew that I was serious when I said that I might drop out of the show because of the gruelling drive to London and back, but she offered a solution.

'I'll come along to help, if you'll let me, and Dave will drive us. He would love to have an excuse to spend the day in London.'

I knew from the tone of her voice that she was completely serious.

'I can't let you both do that – it's just too much – but it's so kind of you to offer,' I replied.

'Of course you can! You can't not go after all you've battled with to get this far! Think about it and phone me back in a few minutes. OK?'

'OK, I will. Thank you.'

I wanted desperately to accept her offer, but I felt bad about letting Dave, Deb's husband, do all the driving. I phoned Deb back and asked if she was really serious.

'Of course I am!' Deb answered. 'You know I am, and I'd love to come with you – it's all so exciting!'

'All right, then,' I gratefully submitted. 'It would be fantastic, but you must let me pay for the petrol.'

'That's settled, then. Now go and get some sleep – don't forget you need to be here by four forty-five in the morning!'

Chandi and I crawled out of bed at 3 a.m. We dragged ourselves to Deb's house and soon we were on our way to London. Chandi and I had no idea what to expect, but I knew that at some point we would be lined up on a stage and told whether or not we had been success-ful. Dave dropped us off outside the Grand Connaught Rooms at 10 a.m. and Deb, Chandi and I were all feeling quite excited and nervous as we made our way into the huge building. After our audition number – a whopping 100,046 – had been checked off a long list, we made our way through hundreds of people to the far side of the enormous room and found a quiet spot away from the lights. We made Chandi comfortable on the bed I had brought for her, and Deb and I grabbed two chairs for ourselves, preparing for a really long wait.

We had been there all of ten minutes when a researcher came over to say that we were needed for some filming. Chandi, Deb and I got up and followed the researcher, weaving our way past all the hundreds of other acts waiting to hear their fate later that day. We reached three empty chairs with lights and a camera crew, and the researcher told me to wait for Ant and Dec, who would be over shortly to interview us. Neither Deb nor I was expecting that, and Deb suddenly seemed to get a little overexcited! It was lovely having Deb with me to share all of this and it made the whole day wonderful. It was a fun interview, with Dec doing most of the talking this time, rather than Ant.

Dec started the interview by telling me how everyone was raving about Chandi and me after our last audition and asked what I thought of that.

I couldn't help but laugh. 'You are joking, aren't you?'

On hearing my reaction, Dec started to laugh too and motioned to the camera with his hand. 'Would I have just said all that on camera if it wasn't true?'

I shrugged and laughed some more. I had no idea whether we were going to make the final cut, and I certainly wasn't going to sit there brimming with confidence. Dec realized that he wasn't going to get a cocky answer out of me and moved the interview on.

The producer wanted some extra footage of Chandi,

so I asked her to look left and then right, much to the amazement of the film crew and Ant and Dec. Chandi was obligingly swinging her head in whichever direction I asked and was enjoying the attention and showing off a little for the camera. Dec watched Chandi carry out all the tiny instructions I gave her and told me that he thought she was amazing. That was one statement I could definitely agree with.

Soon after, Chandi and I joined the second small group of acts to be bussed over to the Vaudeville Theatre on the Strand, where we would finally be told if we had made it through to the live semi-finals. The moment we had been waiting for was here and I felt nervous. I didn't know what to expect, but I kept hoping it was going to be good.

Chandi and I were told to wait in the dark corridor that led down to the stage. There were five other acts anxiously waiting with us. After a few friendly exchanges, no one said a word – we were all too nervous! Four of the acts were singers, and there was one dance act, along with Chandi and me. We filed down onto the stage and waited. The theatre was dark apart from the bright lights that shone directly on those of us waiting. Chandi looked up at me intently, sensing the tension.

Amanda started to speak, but I was finding it difficult to concentrate. Then I heard her say, 'We have seen a lot of dog acts this year.' She paused. 'Some were terrible, others were good, but some . . .' another pause '. . . were outstanding!'

Could that possibly mean me and Chandi? There was another huge, expectant pause and still Chandi looked up at me.

Suddenly Amanda spoke again. 'And you're *all* through!'

I couldn't believe it! I bent down to stroke Chandi and she leaned over and licked my face. The other acts were laughing and crying and hugging each other. Once we had heard the result, we made our way off the stage to the back of the theatre. I started to follow when Simon, who had recovered from man flu, said to me, 'Can I meet Chandi, as I haven't actually seen her yet?'

I agreed and walked to the front of the stage with her. Simon came over and Chandi waited patiently until he had finished stroking her. I was just glad that he seemed to like Chandi, and when Simon had said goodbye, we finally found our way off the stage and out of the back of the auditorium. After I found the correct door, we were hit by bright daylight. I found myself squinting, and Chandi was blinking as much as I was.

When I could look up, I saw Dec was stood right in front of me. Chandi and I had been in the theatre with Simon for so long that they had already talked to the other acts and filmed their reaction to the good news. The camera crew had gone off to film some longer interviews, and so it was just me, Chandi, Ant and Dec stood there. I felt a bit shy at that point, and more so when Dec grabbed my arm very firmly, leaned in, looked me straight in the eye and said, 'Do you believe me now?'

We had made it to the next round and I couldn't deny we had done well. I looked back at him and quietly replied, 'Yes, I believe I do.'

And as the words left my mouth, the moment was over. The door opened in front of us and Chandi and I were asked to go through to our next interview.

The day was far from over for the forty acts that had made it through to the next round of the competition. There were more interviews for ITV2 and then filming of all the acts stood on the stage together, while Ant and Dec filmed their links. Chandi and I were right at the front, since Chandi was definitely the smallest on the stage. I crouched down next to her.

Finally the day was over and Chandi and I were exhausted. We could barely put one foot in front of the other by this point. We finished after 10 p.m. and I was incredibly grateful to remember that I didn't have to drive home. Dave was waiting for us and listened excitedly to the day's events as he drove us all home. When we reached Deb and Dave's, I still had the fifty-minute drive back to our house, so Chandi and I didn't get home until 1.50 a.m. on Saturday. Fortunately Chandi was able to sleep in the car on the way home. It had been an incredibly long and tiring day, but we had made it through!

We had been told at the reveal day that all of the top forty acts would have to return to London for a meeting in two weeks' time, but until then there was time to adjust to the fact that we had been selected to perform on such a major show. I couldn't believe it! Deb and I phoned each other constantly over the next few months. She was so excited for us and offered to come to London for the live semi-final. I was – and still am – extremely grateful for her friendship and support. I hadn't had anyone to share anything with to this extent since my mum had died, and our constant conversations made the build-up to *Britain's Got Talent* even more special.

Three days later, though, Chandi was once again unconscious on the operating table, having the polyp on her leg removed. There was a good reason why it was refusing to heal: it was necrotic, so surgically removing it was the only thing to do.

Twelve

Excitement and Possibilities

'One minute,' said a voice in my ear, and my stomach lurched.

This was only the dress rehearsal, so I told myself not to be stupid. Chandi and I stood on a mark behind the doors, waiting to make our entry. My mind was blank and I felt sick. I looked down and there was Chandi, looking back at me, her eyes sparkling. It was a running joke that Chandi and I had matching buckets backstage and I imagined the two of us with our heads in our designated buckets. I couldn't help but smile at this image, and I relaxed, but only a little.

'Ten, nine, eight, seven, six, five, four, three, two, one,' said Paul, the assistant floor manager, looking intently at me as he counted.

I acknowledged that I was listening and my attention turned to Chandi, while I tried to ignore the somersaulting in my stomach.

'Ready?' I asked.

Chandi winked at me and I smiled back at her.

The huge doors slid open and it was time . . .

In June, four months after our audition in front of Amanda, Louis and Piers, Chandi and I drove to London with Debbie for four days of rehearsals before the live semi-final. *Britain's Got Talent* had put us up in a hotel near the studios.

Chandi, Debbie and I stood in the airless corridor of the Fountain Studios waiting to be called for the dress rehearsal for that evening's second semi-final. I was asking Chandi if she wanted a drink when Debbie nudged me. Ant was striding down the corridor towards us, with Dec swiftly following behind.

As Ant got closer, he nodded in our direction and said in his broad Geordie accent, 'All right?'

Deb and I smiled at him and then our eyes turned to Dec, who smiled widely and crouched down to stroke Chandi. She leaned in close and grinned up at him. Chandi had developed a soft spot for Dec, and it appeared that the feeling was completely mutual. Dec stayed chatting to us and stroking Chandi until Paul insisted that he come into the studio so they could start. Everyone was waiting for him.

'See you in there,' Dec said with a nod and a wink.

After giving Chandi one more pat, he turned and walked into the darkness of the studio. We waited in the corridor outside, where it was cooler. I held an electric fan over Chandi and she closed her eyes as the breeze passed over her face.

I could tell she was conserving her energy for the evening. She had insisted on walking slowly and carefully as we made our way from our dressing room and was very calm and relaxed. The tense atmosphere all around us didn't affect her, but I knew she could sense this was a situation like no other we'd experienced.

We'd won our place on the biggest talent show in television and this was an opportunity for everyone to see exactly how talented Chandi was, above and beyond everything we'd achieved at Crufts. I was also aware of the opportunities that could come after appearing on such a widely viewed show – if the public took a liking to you – and was definitely feeling the pressure. I loved every second of the experience, but I carried an extra responsibility. With Chandi in the mix, my main task was making sure she was comfortable – I refused to allow her to be stressed or overworked, and the production team was kind enough to give us our own dressing room in a Portakabin in a quiet spot. I wanted to put her interests first.

We were called into the studio; just going through

the double doors into the darkness made my stomach lurch. Making sure that Chandi paid attention to the cables strewn across the floor, we made our way to the area behind the stage where I had a few minutes to warm her up before going on. Paul gave us our five-minute call as we went through our pre-performance ritual of some of our favourite moves and I praised Chandi to get her excited. Suddenly I was aware of Paul's countdown and the huge sliding doors out onto the stage opened.

I cued the music by placing my umbrella prop firmly on the floor and we ran through our 'Me and My Shadow' routine, which we'd spent four weeks practising. We had a few timing issues with a new move I called our 'funny walk', and Chandi's ears went down when she realized she'd made a mistake, but I was already helping her before she looked up at me. I gently touched each of her hips in turn to remind her which hind leg she should be lifting and she quickly got back into the routine. It was less than perfect, but we took a bow and waited for Ant and Dec to walk over to talk to us, as they would do in the real show. When Chandi saw Dec coming, she went straight to him, despite me calling her! She glanced over to me but sat herself squarely on Dec's feet, asking for some affection. Dec happily obliged and stroked her while reading his lines from the autocue. Then it was all over until the live show.

When we left the studio, I had some time to think through the performance we'd just given. I wasn't too concerned about the funny walk going a little wrong — we had invented it especially for this routine. It involved Chandi lifting her hind legs in turn and me matching my movements to hers. We both knew she could do it brilliantly, but I was glad of the rehearsal to iron out any issues. Before Chandi rested, we tried the funny walk a couple more times, using my hand to guide her. Everything was going to be fine, I told myself as we walked back to our dressing room with Debbie.

I had every faith in Chandi; we had been in many situations like this over the years and Chandi had *always* risen to the occasion. It wasn't long now until together we would give our biggest performance ever, in front of just over eleven million people.

I couldn't eat anything before the live show, but Chandi wolfed her food down and stretched out contentedly in her bed for a sleep. With two fans blowing on her at full speed, I was relieved that she was comfortable and relaxed enough to snooze. Debbie stayed with her while I went to have my hair and make-up done.

The make-up room was full of noise, with people laughing and chatting while the make-up artists worked on making them look their best. I was glad the chair I was to sit in was in the corner of the room, and as I sat down, the lady doing my make-up asked me if I was feeling all right.

'I'm just a bit nervous,' I replied, trying to underplay it. Truthfully, this was the most petrified I had ever felt before a performance. I briefly wondered what would happen if I were just to leave the building with Chandi and go home. There didn't seem much point in running away, though, so on the advice of the make-up artists I started to take some deep breaths and try to relax.

It seemed like only a few minutes before we were being called for the real live performance. Debbie helped me gather together what we needed for our trip down the corridors to the studio. In our bright pink matching outfits – me in a waistcoat and Chandi in her specially made neck scarf, which we call a Chandana – we made our way past the paparazzi hanging over the twelve-foot-high perimeter fence trying to get a picture.

Thanks to the previous rehearsals, Chandi and I knew how everything was going to work, and that addressed my nerves a little. Before I knew it, it was time for us to go up behind the doors and get Chandi as excited as I could before we walked out in front of the huge studio audience, and millions of people watching at home.

'Ten seconds,' I was told. 'Nine, eight, seven, six, five, four . . .'

'Ready?' I asked.

As usual, Chandi winked at me and I smiled back at her.

'. . . three, two, one . . .'

The huge doors slid open and it was time. We walked forward, side by side, with my umbrella smartly tucked under my arm, and took centre stage. I was just about to position the umbrella on the floor when I heard someone in the audience yell out, 'Go on, Tina!'

My friend Paula worked at the same school as Debbie and me and she had come all the way down to London to support us. It was lovely to hear her voice cheering me on and it boosted my confidence. Taking her advice, I cued the music.

We started and the opening move went well, Chandi lifting her front legs in turn before going into our funny walk. I encouraged Chandi with all my heart and soul and it worked – we were perfectly in time for every lift of our legs! We'd nailed that move! I could hear the audience laugh and applaud through the routine in all the right places and their support made Chandi and me fly through each of the moves. My mouth was dry, and Chandi was panting, but her eyes never left mine.

We were coming to the final moves. Chandi was supposed to run round me, come between my knees, sit up and beg, and then hold the umbrella that I handed her between her front paws. The music and the roar of the audience rose to a deafening crescendo. I told Chandi to get into the beg position, but she didn't stop running round me! I realized that she couldn't hear me, so I shouted to her to 'come through' and at last she heard, got into position and closed her paws round the umbrella on the final chord of the music. I had thought we were going to miss the ending, but we just made it in time and no one knew there had been a problem.

Breathless but beaming, we took a bow and the audience calmed down as Ant and Dec came over. Chandi wagged her tail and leapt around in excitement but then stayed by my side and didn't run over to Dec for a cuddle. She knew this was the real performance and was being very professional. It was time to hear the judges' verdicts. Piers and Amanda both heaped lots of praise on Chandi, but it was Simon's feedback that I anxiously awaited.

Ant said to him, 'Simon, you've never seen Chandi live before because you weren't at the auditions. What did you make of it?'

'I love her!' said Simon, and the audience applauded.

'Which one?' asked Dec.

'Both!' replied Simon.

And with that it was time to leave the stage and wait for the public's verdict on who they wanted in Saturday's final. Deb met us when we came off stage and we made our way back up the stiflingly hot corridor and out to our peaceful Portakabin. Chandi was glad to see her bed again and got in it straight away. I poured her another drink and held the bowl for her. After a few gulps, she raised her head, licked my thumb, looking up at me with the softest expression, and blinked her eyes slowly before swallowing. She didn't need words to thank me for looking after her; everything she did said it all.

I was still energized from the excitement of performing, but relieved that it was over and we could now relax a bit. I was satisfied we had given it our best; now we just had to wait. Only two acts would go forward to Saturday's final: the winner of the public vote would go straight through, and the judges would then consider the acts that came second and third in the vote and choose between them.

After thirty minutes, they called us back to the studio for the results show. Chandi and I were again stood on the stage, but this time with the rest of that night's acts, waiting to hear Ant and Dec announce the winner of the public vote. I didn't for one second think it would be us. Nevertheless, after the big build-up and the customary pause to build tension, Dec shouted, 'Tina and Chandi!'

We had won the public vote! I was absolutely stunned and couldn't remember what they'd told us during rehearsal about being the winning act. Was I supposed to walk off? I headed to the left of the stage with Chandi, but as I walked away, I wondered if I was supposed to have said or done something first. In any case, no one stopped us and it was too late to worry.

Then came an anxious moment for the two acts with the next highest number of votes, as the judges decided who went through to the final. Chandi and I stood on the side of the stage away from the cameras while the judges voted. Chandi wouldn't sit still, though, and kept trying to go back to the centre of the stage! She obviously liked it there.

While we were waiting, I was overwhelmed with gratitude to everyone who had picked up the phone to vote for us. Thanks to them, we had achieved what I dared not dream about – we had made it to the final. I found out a few days later that we had received 58.1 per cent of the vote that night, which turned out to be the second highest public vote of the entire series.

When the second place had been decided, we walked back on stage to stand next to Ant and Dec while they brought the show to a close. After saying his final piece to camera, Dec turned to me and gave me the biggest hug, while the audience cheered and the *Britain's Got Talent* music signalled the end of the show.

Waking up the next morning was difficult. After the previous night's excitement, Chandi and I went back to the hotel with Debbie. One of Debbie's sons, Jake, joined us there too, as did her sister, Teri – they had also come to London to offer support. Back in our room, I got straight on to the computer, anxious to check our Facebook page and new website. I had set them up a few months before, just in case things went well for us on the show, and I couldn't believe the sheer volume of positive comments that had been left for us that day. I tried to read them all, soaking up the whole amazing experience, and it took me hours. Chandi happily dropped off to sleep, but only when I couldn't keep my eyes open any longer did I go to bed. It was a very late night.

I was woken up by the sound of someone banging on my door. I glanced down at Chandi, but she was still asleep, lying on her back in her bed with her paws waving in the air. When I rolled out of bed and fumbled my way to the door, it turned out to be Debbie, looking like death warmed up. Apparently, the ITV press office had been on the phone – Chandi and I were needed for press interviews and a photo call in an hour's time. It was just gone 8.30 a.m.

I pulled myself together and we made our way to a nearby hotel, ready for a long day. As Chandi, Deb and I left our hotel, though, people kept coming over to con-gratulate us and stroke Chandi, and I could tell she was getting a bit tired of the attention. When we reached the hotel where the interviews were being held, there was a bigger crowd of people outside who rushed at us waving camera phones when we got out of the car. I wasn't expecting any of this!

It felt like coming out of a protective bubble into the real world. I was concerned for Chandi, as everyone just lunged forward to touch her, so I put myself in front and moved us away with the help of Ellen from the ITV press office and two of the hotel porters. We whisked Chandi straight into the waiting lift and up and away from the craziness to meet with the journalists. I breathed a sigh of relief in the lift and looked at Debbie.

'What have I done?' I asked her in a slightly anxious voice.

'Don't worry,' she said, shaking her head slightly. 'It'll be fine.'

After a series of back-to-back interviews with different newspapers, we went outside for photos. Chandi posed for the photographers for a short while until the sweltering heat made me bring things to a close. It had been a whirlwind of a day.

When I had the chance to think, I remembered that we were only partway through *Britain's Got Talent* and that making it to the final meant we had one more routine to prepare for, and it was just four days away. While I had some preliminary ideas, it hadn't seemed possible to plan that far ahead and I only had the bare bones of a routine. I had to start work, though, and soon, otherwise we wouldn't be ready in time. We were given a large room at the hotel to rehearse in, and with the help of my portable CD player and Debbie's watchful eye, Chandi and I started to put together the routine for Saturday.

I had originally wanted to do the ballet routine if we made it to the final, but Chandi had suffered an injury out on a walk in early March, just a few weeks after our second audition. I had dropped my scarf and when I asked Chandi to get it for me, she had run full tilt towards it and not slowed down as she turned to pick it up, so her whole body had flipped a full 180 degrees, leaving her spreadeagled on the ground. I could feel nothing obviously wrong and she got up and seemed fine, so we went home. Two days later, though, Chandi had been struggling to move about and looked like she was in pain. Our McTimoney chiropractor, Harriet, had told us she had misaligned her spine and pelvis. She treated Chandi, but the problem persisted for many weeks and she associated the discomfort of her pelvis being misaligned with the hind-leg moves. I could clearly see how wary she was of hind-leg moves, even once she was well again, and I didn't want her to do anything she was reluctant to do. Even though I was bitterly disappointed at not being able to include any of these amazing moves, I stopped even attempting them with Chandi.

I needed a routine for the final that would look fabulous even without our signature moves. I had taken all the beautiful hind-leg moves out of the 'Me and My Shadow' routine, but the public didn't seem to care, as we had won our semi-final!

Encouraged by this, I focused on using props to make our final routine the best it could be without any hind-leg moves. I chose the song 'Let's Face the Music and Dance' and we worked on a move where Chandi rips off my trouser leg and another cute move where Chandi rests her front paws on the seat of a chair to hide her eyes. It looks as though she's crying just as the song mentions teardrops.

We rehearsed for several hours each day before the final and Deb tirelessly worked the CD player and helped me with the props. She also dealt with all the phone calls we'd been getting since the start of the show, only interrupting our rehearsals when it was something that only I could deal with. I don't know how I would have managed without her. She was there for me in every way, including sitting for several hours gluing Swarovski crystals onto the lapels of my white satin tailcoat the night before the final. When Deb finally left my room that evening, she really didn't look very well and I was worried about her. I was glad that Dave, her husband, had arrived at the hotel with Jake and her other son, Toby, and they would be with her.

Early the next morning, Chandi and I made our way to the studios for the 9.30 a.m. start. We stopped by Debbie's room first, only to discover that she had been very ill in the night. I felt so sorry for her, but I had to leave and go to the studios. I hated that she would miss out on the experience, especially after all she had done to help us. Dave offered to come for a couple of hours instead, and I was grateful to have him there, but I so missed Debbie, who could read my mind. She was always one step ahead, seeing whatever needed to be done and just doing it.

I tried to focus, but the first rehearsal went badly because I forgot the routine. The dress rehearsal went slightly better, which lifted my spirits a little, but when Debbie arrived just an hour before the live show, I burst into tears. Even though she was not completely well, she had struggled to be there for me, as she said she would, and it meant the world to me.

I was still incredibly nervous when the doors slid open and Chandi and I walked onto the stage for our performance in the final, but I took a deep breath, shot Chandi a smile and gave it my all. The music started and Chandi performed every move on cue. It was unbelievable just to be there together, and at the end of the routine, Chandi wagged her tail furiously as I told her how good she had been and how proud I was.

In the end, we came fourth in the final of *Britain's Got Talent* and I couldn't have been happier. Out of the thousands of people who had auditioned, Chandi and I had made it to the final and shared the most amazing experience. I was excited about the future and the opportunities it could hold for us both.

Epilogue

When *Britain's Got Talent* was finally over, it was very hard to resume a normal routine without feeling a bit flat. We only had two weeks at home, though, before more adventure, as Chandi and I joined the *Britain's Got Talent* Live Tour with the nine other acts from the final. It was very humbling thinking about the number of people who must have picked up the phone to vote for us. I felt so much gratitude for each and every vote cast for us, and still do. Thanks to all those votes, the next few months were very exciting.

The tour took us all around the UK, and Chandi enjoyed the applause of many more audiences in major venues up and down the country. We even managed to squeeze in a spot of live television in Glasgow for Scottish TV's *The Hour*, giving an interview and performance of 'Me and My Shadow' to promote the tour.

It had been months since I had asked Chandi to

perform her hind-leg moves, but we tried them out in the rehearsal, just for fun, and to my delight Chandi was as keen as ever to try and performed everything I asked, including our beloved back-to-back move, with ease and gusto. We performed our 'Me and My Shadow' routine with the choreography I had originally planned for *Britain's Got Talent* on *The Hour* and then for the last seven performances of the tour, including at Wembley and the O2 Arena. Whenever Chandi stood up on her hind legs, the audience would start to scream and cheer with appreciation, which was an amazing feeling.

After the tour finished, offers came in via our new management team, and after several live performances at events around the country, we were invited to appear on *This Morning*, *BBC Breakfast* and BBC London's radio show *Barking at the Moon*. Chandi and I were invited to the premiere of *Cats & Dogs 2: The Revenge of Kitty Galore*, and we experienced what it was like to walk down the red carpet together and have our photo taken like celebrities. We were also invited to a *Dogs Today* photo shoot; in fact Chandi and I were the cover stars for the following month's edition of the magazine, making another of my dreams come true.

Just before the tour, we were approached by a company that makes many of the DVDs for the top celebrities in the country and I was given the chance to present my own DVD with the best co-host ever – Chandi. We filmed it over two days in October and did a staggering amount of press to promote it, including local radio interviews, *The Alan Titchmarsh Show*, *Daybreak*, *This Week*, where Chandi did her own special review of 2010, and *BBC Breakfast* once more. Each time Chandi has shown how happy she is to perform and how much she loves working with me in her enthusiastic routines, despite some difficult working conditions!

When I first met Chandi, I was attracted by her striking markings and a sense that we were supposed to be together, but I had no idea how strong our relationship would become, or of the adventures we were to share.

The love I have for Chandi, and still have for Pepper, even though I can't see her any longer, transcends the physical body. They are my family, pure and simple. The devotion, loyalty and love that they have shown me are so precious and extraordinary, and I give it all back in equal measure. When I look at Chandi, I look into her soul and the goodness inside her.

When people see Chandi and me together, the first thing they comment on is the fact that Chandi rarely takes her eyes off me. She will let other people stroke her, but she never looks at them for more than a few seconds.

She looks at me when I'm driving, and if I hold out my hand, she will rest her fuzzy little chin in my upturned palm. The way she licks my thumb after I've held her water bowl for her to take a drink and then blinks very slowly at me, and the times she gently touches her nose on my leg to tell me she loves me, and gazes up at me, melt my heart every time. The look of excitement on her face when I ask her if she wants to skip with me is wonderful, as she rushes to get into position next to my left leg, her mouth hanging open in a huge grin, both of us completely caught up in the moment.

Being with Chandi is a pure joy. It is uncomplicated and makes me feel so complete. I've talked about our achievements and the fantastic experiences we have shared, but what I treasure most is the incredible bond between us, something I longed for as a child. I truly believe she is my soul mate.

The greatest thing that all the experiences of my life have taught me is to be 'present' in every moment of every day. All we have is here and now, and to spend the present time worrying about the future or regretting the past is pointless, and a complete waste of life. I treasure each day that Chandi and I share, and we make the most of the time we have together, whether it's raining or the sun is shining. We make sure we have adventures at every opportunity, even when an adventure doesn't look likely.

As a result, I have a lifetime of precious memories and shared moments stored in my head that I can dive into at any moment.

We only have a short time to dance on the earth, and together, Chandi and I truly dance with all our heart and soul. I try not to think about the future and the day, like Pepper before her, Chandi has to leave our dance. But the dance can't end while the music is still playing . . .

Picture credits

All photographs are from the author's personal collection with the following exceptions:

Page 3 middle: © Tim Rose for *Dogs Today*

Page 4 middle: courtesy of Roy Anderson

Page 5: © www.actionshots.me.uk

Page 6 top: © McClure Photography, www.mcclurephotography.co.uk

Page 7: © Ken McKay/Talkback Thames/Rex Features

www.panmacmillan.com